The restricted hospital order: from court to the community

by
Robert Street

A Research and Statistics Directorate Report

Home Office
Research and
Statistics
Directorate

London: Home Office

Home Office Research Studies

The Home Office Research Studies are reports on research undertaken by or on behalf of the Home Office. They cover the range of subjects for which the Home Secretary has responsibility. Titles in the series are listed at the back of this report (copies are available from the address on the back cover). Other publications produced by the Research and Statistics Directorate include Research Findings, the Research Bulletin, Statistical Bulletins and Statistical Papers.

The Research and Statistics Directorate

The Directorate consists of Units which deal with research and statistics on Crime and Criminal Justice, Offenders and Corrections, Immigration and General Matters; the Programme Development Unit; the Economics Unit; and the Operational Research Unit.

The Research and Statistics Directorate is an integral part of the Home Office, serving the Ministers and the department itself, its services, Parliament and the public through research, development and statistics. Information and knowledge from these sources informs policy development and the management of programmes; their dissemination improves wider public understanding of matters of Home Office concern.

First published 1998

Application for reproduction should be made to the Information and Publications Group, Room 201, Home Office, 50 Queen Anne's Gate, London SW1H 9AT.

©Crown copyright 1998 ISBN 1 84082 126 4
ISSN 0072 6435

Foreword

Under section 41 of the Mental Health Act 1983, judges are entitled to impose restriction orders on convicted mentally disordered offenders, following the decision to send those offenders to hospital for treatment. Such orders have the effect of placing constraints upon the transfer and discharge of offenders from hospital, and seek to ensure continuing treatment, supervision, and monitoring once offenders are released from hospital.

As restricted hospital orders not only play an important role in protecting the public from potentially dangerous mentally disordered offenders, but can also have significant implications for the civil liberties of such offenders, it is important that they are used appropriately.

In an attempt to assess the effectiveness of restricted hospital orders, as well as provide more information about their use, this study looked a the characteristics of a sample of offenders who were made subject to these orders, and examined the progress of a sample of restricted patients who were discharged from hospital. It found that, on the whole, the orders were effective. They were imposed upon offenders who generally presented sufficient evidence to be considered as posing a risk of serious harm to others. The great majority of those discharged were not convicted of further offences that caused or threatened harm to others.

DAVID MOXON
Head of the Crime and Criminal Justice Unit
Research and Statistics Directorate

Acknowledgements

Thanks are due to a number of people who contributed in a variety of ways to this project. Liz Butler, Steve Goodman, Jessica Harris, Sarah Hitchcock, Ben Moxon, and Celeste Pattaralowha diligently collected the data from MHU files. All the interview respondents were extremely generous with their time, as were the staff from the two MHRT areas I visited in helping set up the interviews with tribunal members. Last but not least, a number of Home Office colleagues from RSD and MHU, but especially Carol Hedderman, Nigel Shackleford and David Brown, gave invaluable advice and assistance.

Contents

Summary

Introduction

Most mentally disordered people do not offend and of those who do, most do not do so seriously. However, there is a small group of mentally disordered offenders who present a risk of serious harm to the public. In such cases, following the decision to order the offender's detention in hospital, a judge is also empowered under Section 41 of the Mental Health Act (MHA) 1983 to impose a restriction order. The aim of a restriction order is to protect the public by placing constraints upon the transfer and discharge of that offender from hospital.

Restricted patients can be subsequently discharged from hospital either with the agreement of the Home Secretary or by a Mental Health Review Tribunal (MHRT). Discharge is usually granted on a conditional basis, enabling patients' continuing treatment, supervision and monitoring in the community. The Home Secretary retains the power to recall any conditionally discharged patient to hospital.

Because of the far-reaching consequences of such orders (which are usually made for an indefinite period) upon the offender and the fact that their enforcement is very resource-intensive, it is important that restriction orders are used only where appropriate and that they are not kept in place longer than is necessary. Furthermore, it is also necessary to gauge their effectiveness in protecting the public. The Home Office's Mental Health Unit (MHU) commissioned research to examine these issues.

Firstly, the study examined the characteristics of those offenders who had restricted hospital orders imposed at court in 1992 and 1993. Secondly, it looked at those patients on restricted hospital orders first discharged from hospital between 1987 and 1990, following their progress in the community through until the end of 1994. The principal outcomes of interest here were reconviction and recall to hospital.

Section 1: the imposition of restriction orders

The sample comprised 372 offenders who received hospital orders with restrictions at court in 1992 and 1993. Data were collected from offenders' MHU files and supplemented by interviews with seven judges and six forensic psychiatrists.

Details of the sample

- Most of the sample (77%) were diagnosed as being mentally ill; 13 per cent were diagnosed as being psychopathically disordered (PD); six per cent as mentally impaired and the remaining four per cent as being mentally ill *and* psychopathically disordered (MI + PD).

- All but six per cent of the restriction orders were imposed without limit of time. The average length of time-limited orders was five years. Those given time-limited orders tended to have been convicted of less serious offences than those given indefinite orders.

- Just under half of the sample were convicted of either manslaughter, attempted murder or assaults causing grievous bodily harm (GBH), and a further quarter were convicted of either sexual offences or arson.

- Fifty-three per cent of victims were either partners, other family members, friends or acquaintances. A third of the victims were strangers and 14 per cent were officials (usually a police officer, nurse or doctor). There was no immediate victim in a tenth of cases, usually where the index offence was arson.

- Most offenders (74%) had a criminal record when the restriction order was imposed, including 47 per cent who had previous convictions for sexual or violent offences. Two–fifths of the sample had previously served a custodial sentence.

- The majority of the sample (69%) had been psychiatric in-patients before and of those, 65 per cent had been compulsorily detained under a section of the Mental Health Act.

- Eighty-eight per cent of the sample were men. Men were less likely than women to be diagnosed as PD, but more likely to be diagnosed as mentally ill. There were also differences between the sexes in terms of index offence, previous convictions and previous psychiatric history.

- There were notable differences between the diagnostic groups in terms of the nature of the index offence and ethnicity of the offenders.

- There was a relatively high proportion of black offenders, comprising 21 per cent of the sample for whom ethnicity data was available (and 19% of the total sample).

Psychiatrists' risk assessments and recommendations

- Seventy per cent of offenders were described by a majority of the psychiatric reports in their case as presenting a risk to others. Those who had committed the most serious index offences were the most likely to be described as a risk.

- Restriction orders were only expressly recommended by a majority of psychiatric reports in 41 per cent of cases, although doctors often mentioned restriction orders as a possibility for the court to decide upon or recommended a hospital order in conditions of high security. Only one per cent of reports expressly opposed a restriction order.

Comparisons with offenders who received unrestricted hospital orders

- A comparison of the sample group with offenders who received unrestricted hospital orders in 1992 and 1993 (the control group) revealed that the sample group were significantly more likely to have been convicted of a serious index offence (violent or sexual offences and arson), while the control group were more likely to have been convicted of either offences against property (excluding arson) or public order offences.

- The sample group were also significantly more likely to have previous convictions for violence, although there was no difference between the two groups in terms of having previous convictions for any type of offence, or previous custodial sentences.

- Some of the control group were convicted of very serious index offences, and some of the sample group were convicted of less serious offences, illustrating that restriction orders are imposed on the basis of perceived risk and not just harm caused.

Interviews with judges and psychiatrists

- All respondents thought that restriction orders generally worked well. Judges tended to see the orders predominantly in terms of securely detaining an offender in hospital, while psychiatrists focused more on longer term supervision and treatment.

Section 2: a follow-up of restricted patients discharged into the community

The second part of the study focused upon the 391 patients detained on restricted hospital orders who were first discharged from hospital between 1987 and 1990, focusing principally on any reconvictions and recalls to hospital up until the end of 1994. In addition eight members of Mental Health Review Tribunals and five members of the Home Office Mental Health Unit were interviewed.

Details of the sample

- The patients' restriction orders had been imposed between 1961 and 1989, with three-fifths of the sample being sentenced under the 1959, rather than the 1983, MHA.

- The majority (64%) had been detained under the MHA category of mental illness; a further 24 per cent were classified as being psychopathically disordered, ten per cent as mentally impaired and three per cent were detained under mixed MHA categories.

- Eighty-three per cent of the patients were male. Of the cases where ethnicity was known, 15 per cent were black; 81 per cent were white and the remaining four per cent were Asian or from another ethnic group.

- Almost half the index offences were either manslaughter, attempted murder or causing GBH. A further 14 per cent had been convicted of a sexual offence and 17 per cent were convicted of arson.

- Seventy per cent of the patients already had a criminal record when their restriction order was imposed. Of these, 61 per cent (43% of the total sample) had a conviction for a previous violent or sexual offence.

- Two-thirds had been in-patients before their restriction orders were imposed.

Discharge from hospital

- Ninety-five per cent of the sample were conditionally discharged from hospital; the other five per cent were absolutely discharged. Nearly two-thirds (62%) of patients were discharged by a MRHT, the remainder with the consent of the Home Office.

- Patients had spent an average of nearly nine years detained in hospital before discharge. Mentally impaired patients spent longer in hospital on average than mentally ill or psychopathically disordered patients.

- Home Office discharges usually followed the receipt of favourable reports from those caring for the patient. The principal reason for MHRT discharges (given in 86% of cases) was that the patient's disorder was not of a nature or degree warranting detention.

- The Home Office, in its statement to the tribunal, opposed discharge in 86 per cent of MHRT cases, but strong opposition was expressed in only 6 per cent.

- Patients in the mental illness category were more likely to be discharged by the Home Office, while those in the mental impairment and PD categories were more likely to be discharged by a MHRT.

Circumstances following discharge

- Details were only available for the 370 conditionally discharged patients. Over half of these were initially discharged to a group home or hostel. Following discharge, about one-third of patients formed a relationship with a partner and the majority enjoyed at least some social contact with friends, family or other acquaintances.

- Seventy per cent of patients were on psychiatric medication for at least some of their conditional discharge. The mental state of 40 per cent of patients deteriorated to the stage where some psychiatric intervention was required: over a third of patients had a non-recall admission to hospital.

- Nearly one-third of patients caused problems while under supervision. A quarter of patients abused drugs or alcohol at some stage during their conditional discharge.

- Thirteen per cent of patients reported being victimised during the follow-up period, most commonly involving violent or sexual offences.

- Four patients killed themselves and another 43 deliberately harmed themselves.

- By the end of the follow-up, 45 per cent of the conditionally discharged patients were no longer under restrictions, the majority of those having been absolutely discharged by a MHRT.

Reconviction

- Five per cent of the total sample (conditionally and absolutely discharged patients) were reconvicted of serious offences (violent offences, threats to kill, sexual offences, arson, abduction and aggravated burglary) by the end of December 1994. Overall, 12 per cent of the sample were reconvicted of any type of offence.

- Of the three main MHA categories, PD patients were the most likely to be reconvicded of either a serious offence or any type of offence, although this was not a statistically significant variation (possibly because the numbers involved were so small).

- There was no difference between MHRT and Home Office discharges in terms of reconvictions for serious offences.

- Serious reconvictions were more likely in cases where there were previous convictions for sexual or violent offences (particularly previous sexual offences). Patients whose supervisors expressed concerns about the risk or the problems they presented were more likely to have been reconvicted for a serious offence.

- Patients who miused alcohol or drugs or who suffered a deterioration in their mental state that required intervention were also more likely to have been reconvicted of a serious offence.

Harmful incidents

- In addition to reconvictions, 13 per cent of conditionally discharged patients were reportedly involved in incidents that were harmful (or potentially harmful) to others but did not result in conviction. However, over a third of the incidents did lead to recall to hospital.

- As with reconvictions, patients who caused problems with their supervision, abused drugs or alcohol, or whose mental state deteriorated while in the community were more likely to be involved in harmful incidents. There was a significant association between involvement in these incidents and being reconvicted of a serious offence.

Recall

- A quarter of conditionally discharged patients were recalled to hospital during the follow-up period (including 5% who were recalled on more than one occasion).

- Concern about mental state was the most common reason for recall, although concerns about risk (often following reported incidents of dangerous behaviour) featured in over half of recalls.

- By the end of the follow-up just over three-quarters of those recalled had been discharged from hospital again. They had spent an average of 15 months in hospital.

Interviews with MHU staff and MHRT members

- MHU and MHRT members, though positive about the restriction order system, shared a number of concerns about the discharge process.

- There were differences between MHU and MHRT respondents on some issues - such as the preferred extent of a tribunal's involvement in restricted cases and the format of the Home Office statement which is submitted to the tribunal. Such divergences of opinion largely reflected the circumstances of having two different organisations taking different approaches to the same goal (discharging restricted patients from hospital safely and effectively).

Discussion

- The study revealed a number of indications of the restricted hospital order's value and effectiveness: firstly, the reconviction rate for serious offences among the sample of discharged patients was very low; secondly, the order helps share the responsibility for the appropriate disposal and management of dangerous mentally disordered offenders between different agencies and decision-makers; and thirdly, for the great majority of the sample such an order seemed the only suitable sentence – prison or unrestricted hospital orders would have been inappropriate.

- However, there were also signs of some possible shortcomings in the operation of restricted hospital orders. In particular: firstly, that in a few cases restriction orders may be imposed too readily; secondly, information available to decision-makers on the index offence, offending history and any dangerous behaviour post-discharge was not always sufficiently detailed; and thirdly, there were indications of a need for continuing if not increasing level of dialogue between the Home Office and MHRTs.

Introduction

Background to the study

Under section 37 of the Mental Health Act (MHA) 1983, a court can order an offender to be detained in a psychiatric hospital for treatment. If, having regard to the nature of the offence, the offender's antecedents, and the risk of further offending, he or she is also considered to pose a risk of serious harm to the public, a judge also has the power to impose a restriction order under section 41. This places constraints upon the offender's transfer, leave of absence and discharge from hospital. Restriction orders can be made for finite periods, but the great majority are made without limit of time. Restriction directions, which have the same effect as a restriction order, can be imposed upon mentally disordered prisoners who are transferred to hospital (under sections 47 and 48 MHA 1983), or offenders who are either found to be unfit to plead, or not guilty by reason of insanity.

On average, just under 200 restriction orders[1] have been imposed at the Crown Court annually over the last decade up to 1996 (Home Office, 1997a), although the numbers have fluctuated during this period: from 154 orders in 1990, to 251 in 1994, and 205 in 1995. Patients on restricted hospital orders comprise the majority (in recent years, about two-thirds) of the total number of restricted patients detained in hospital (Home Office, 1997a).

Recent research indicating that there may be a link between some types or aspects of mental disorder and violence (Hodgins, 1993), together with a number of incidents in which mentally disordered people have caused serious or fatal injuries to members of the public, have highlighted the need for this sort of indeterminate protective order. However, their indeterminacy also makes them open to criticism on civil liberties grounds, as an offender is being detained for what they might do rather than for what they have done. In some cases this type of order may well lead to an offender being detained for longer than if he or she had been sentenced to a term of imprisonment. Writers such as Robertson (1989) have noted that the restriction order essentially represents a compromise between securely detaining those mentally disordered offenders believed to be dangerous and ensuring that they receive necessary psychiatric treatment, an approach which can lead to tensions between clinical and criminal justice objectives.

---

1   This report focuses upon restricted hospital orders made under sections 37 and 41 MHA 1983. As a restriction order cannot be imposed in court without a hospital order being imposed first, the term 'restriction order' is sometimes used in this report as shorthand for 'restricted hospital order'.

There are two ways in which a restricted patient can be discharged from hospital.

- with the consent of the Home Secretary (under section 42(2) MHA 1983), which will be granted if he receives a recommendation to discharge a patient from the patient's Responsible Medical Officer (RMO) and is satisfied that this advice can safely be accepted. This power is entirely discretionary and may be exercised at any time. The Home Secretary may seek the opinions of the Advisory Board on Restricted Patients, a body comprising a number of senior judicial, psychiatric, and lay members, similar to the Parole Board

- by a Mental Health Review Tribunal (MHRT). MHRTs are independent decision-making bodies which come under the authority of the Department of Health. They are composed of three members: a medical member (doctor), a lay member (with relevant experience of mental health issues) and a legal member, who also presides over the hearing. For restricted cases, the legal member has to be either a circuit judge or a recorder. Restricted patients have a yearly statutory entitlement to a MHRT hearing. A MHRT is obliged[2] to order the discharge of a restricted patient if certain statutory conditions are met, namely:

  (a) the MHRT is satisfied that the patient is not suffering from any form or degree of mental disorder which makes continued detention in hospital for treatment necessary

  or

  (b) the MHRT is satisfied that it is not necessary for the health and safety of the patient or the protection of others for hospital detention to continue.

If, in addition, the MHRT is satisfied that it is not appropriate for a patient to remain liable to recall to hospital for further treatment, it must direct that the patient is not only discharged from hospital, but is also absolutely discharged from the terms of his or her restriction order[3].

In practice, absolute discharges from hospital are rare. Most patients released are made subject to a conditional discharge, whereby they are usually subject to a condition of residence and continue to receive supervision from a psychiatrist, and a social worker or probation officer. The purpose of this supervision is to protect the public by assisting with the patient's safe return to the community, and monitoring the patient's mental state and degree of

2   Under section 72(1)(b) MHA 1983.
3   Under section 73(1)(b) MHA 1983.

risk he or she poses to others[4]. The Home Office retains a responsibility for monitoring the supervision of conditionally discharged restricted patients, and under section 42(3) MHA 1983, the Home Secretary has the discretionary power to recall any such patient to hospital.

As restriction orders are imposed specifically to protect the public from serious harm (i.e. on forensic, rather than clinical, criteria), reoffending by discharged restricted patients is obviously of paramount interest. Published statistics show that while some restricted patients do reoffend seriously following discharge from hospital, the great majority do not: over the period 1972[o]–1990, just five per cent of restricted patients were reconvicted of 'grave offences' (i.e. those with a maximum possible sentence of life imprisonment) within five years of their first discharge from hospital (Home Office, 1997b).

There is an extensive body of literature, both American and British, focusing upon the follow-up of discharged psychiatric patients in the community (see Bailey and MacCulloch, 1992, and Murray, 1989, for summaries of the findings). A question addressed by much of this research has been whether (and how) future risk among such patients can be assessed accurately. Both Peay (1989) and Murray (1989) have argued that the only way to justify preventive detention is to show that the risk of reoffending is a real one and that the risk can be assessed accurately. Being unable accurately to predict reoffending among patients discharged from hospital could lead to unacceptably high numbers of both 'false negatives' (patients whose risk of reoffending is predicted to be low but who do reoffend) and 'false positives' (patients whose risk of reoffending is predicted to be high but who do not reoffend).

The problems of accurate risk assessment have been well documented by writers such as Monahan and Steadman (1994). They include: statistical problems associated with predicting the likelihood of rare events, such as serious reoffending; difficulties in drawing general conclusions from a diverse range of studies conducted on many different populations; and unsatisfactory criterion (outcome) and predictor variables. Despite these difficulties, the importance of ensuring that the discharge from hospital of psychiatric patients who have previously offended is as safe and effective as possible means that the search for successful strategies of risk assessment and prediction continues to be pursued.

However, the issue of risk is of course not confined to the question of discharge from hospital. Because of the changes to a patient's circumstances

---

4   Since the period covered by this report there have a number of changes in the implementation of after-care for psychiatric patients discharged from detention for treatment. In 1994, supervision registers were introduced to ensure the identification of all patients thought to pose a significant risk to themselves or others. Then in 1995, the Department of Health took action to ensure that the Care Programme Approach, under which statutory after-care is provided to discharged patients, was being fully implemented.

after release and the unpredictable influence of situational factors, the real test of a patient's propensity to cause harm comes only after time in the community. This highlights that risk assessment at time of discharge is just one part of the overall management of risk in restricted patients.

The close monitoring of restricted patients by the Home Office' Mental Health Unit (MHU), reviews of detention by the Home Secretary and Mental Health Review Tribunals (MHRTs), and supervision on release, mean that restriction orders can be costly to enforce. This, together with the significant (and often long term) constraints that a restriction order places upon patients, make it important to ensure that restriction orders are used appropriately and that they do help ensure public safety. With this in mind, the MHU commissioned research focusing on four main questions:

- who receives restriction orders?

- are they being imposed appropriately?

- how are restricted patients being discharged from hospital?

- what happened to those patients who are discharged in terms of reoffending and recall to hospital?

To answer these questions, a two-part research study was carried out. Part one examined the characteristics of those offenders who had received restriction orders at court in 1992 and 1993. The second part then looked at the decision to discharge restricted patients from hospital, and the patients' subsequent progress in the community.

Methodology

Information was extracted about a sample of 372 offenders given restricted hospital orders in 1992 and 1993⁵. The sample was compiled from lists of names supplied by Home Office sources, and data were collected from the offenders' MHU files.

In addition, a sample of offenders who were given unrestricted hospital orders in 1992 and 1993 was extracted from the Offenders Index (the Home Office's computerised criminal records data base) to discover how far restricted and unrestricted mentally disordered offenders differ in terms of age, sex, index offence and criminal history.

5   The sample was based on information obtained before changes were introduced to the way in which Home Office data on restricted patients were compiled. More recent Home Office figures suggest a total of 416 offenders receiving section 37/41 orders at court in 1992 and 1993 (Home Office 1997a), meaning that the sample for this study represents 89 per cent of that total. There was nothing to suggest any systematic bias in why some cases were excluded from the sample list.

4

These data were supplemented by semi-structured interviews with a number of judges and forensic psychiatrists on issues relating to the process of imposing restriction orders and the use of these orders generally.

In the second part of the study, 391 restricted patients who were first discharged from hospital between 1987 and 1990 were followed up, either until their absolute discharge from the terms of their restriction order, or until the end of December 1994 (for those who had not been absolutely discharged). Discharges from 1987–1990 were chosen so as to allow a follow-up period of at least four years. Again, the principal source of information was MHU files.

The principal outcomes of interest were reoffending and recall to hospital, although a variety of information relating to patients' circumstances following discharge was collected, including information on any harmful incidents that the patient was allegedly involved in and for which he or she was not convicted. A similar, although not identical, measure of 'dangerous incidents' was used by Dell and Grounds (1995) in their study of conditionally discharged patients.

To ensure continuity with the first part of the study, the patients in the sample had all been in hospital under restriction orders imposed at court (under sections 37 and 41 MHA 1983, or their 1959 MHA equivalent). Restricted patients transferred to hospital from prison after sentence, and those detained under the provisions of the Criminal Procedures (Insanity) Act 1964 and Criminal Procedure (Insanity and Unfitness to Plead) Act 1991, were excluded.

The data collected from Home Office files were supplemented by semi-structured interviews with Home Office MHU staff, and members of MHRTs. These covered matters relating to the discharge of restricted patients from hospital, and their subsequent supervision and management in the community.

Section one:
The imposition of restriction orders

8

1 Description of the sample

This chapter describes a sample of 372 offenders who, following the imposition of a hospital order, had a restriction order imposed at the Crown Court under section 41 MHA 1983 in 1992 or 1993 (see footnote 5 on page 4), looking principally at their MHA categories and diagnosis, index offences and criminal records, demographic characteristics and psychiatric histories.

Details of the restriction orders

The orders were imposed at Crown Court centres nationwide, although they were concentrated in major population centres. Nearly a quarter of all the orders were imposed at courts in London.

Only 23 offenders (6%) received time-limited orders, ranging in length from one to seven years (the average being five years). These offenders were more likely to have been convicted of less serious forms of assault or of robbery than those given indefinite restriction orders. They were less likely to have been convicted of serious violence or arson. Overall, those offenders given time-limited orders were significantly[6] less likely to have caused death than those given indefinite orders (none versus 17%), or to have caused actual injury (31% versus 52%).

The time-limited group were only slightly (and not significantly) less likely to have had a previous conviction for a violent or sexual offence. There were also no significant differences between the two groups in terms of sex, diagnosis, and extent of previous psychiatric treatment.

Type of mental disorder

When the restriction orders were imposed, just over three-quarters of the sample (77%) were detained under the MHA category of mental illness; 12 per cent were detained under the category of psychopathic disorder; and five percent under mental impairment (no-one was detained under the category of severe mental impairment). Twenty people (5%) were detained under the dual category of mental illness and psychopathic disorder (MI + PD).

As MHA categories reflect legal rather than psychiatric classifications of mental disorder, a principal diagnosis was also constructed for each case[7]. As this probably reflects a more accurate picture of mental state, it was used in subsequent analyses for any comparisons by type of disorder (including for data featured in Appendices A to C). These main diagnosis groups are shown below in Figure 1.1.

Figure 1.1 Type of disorder

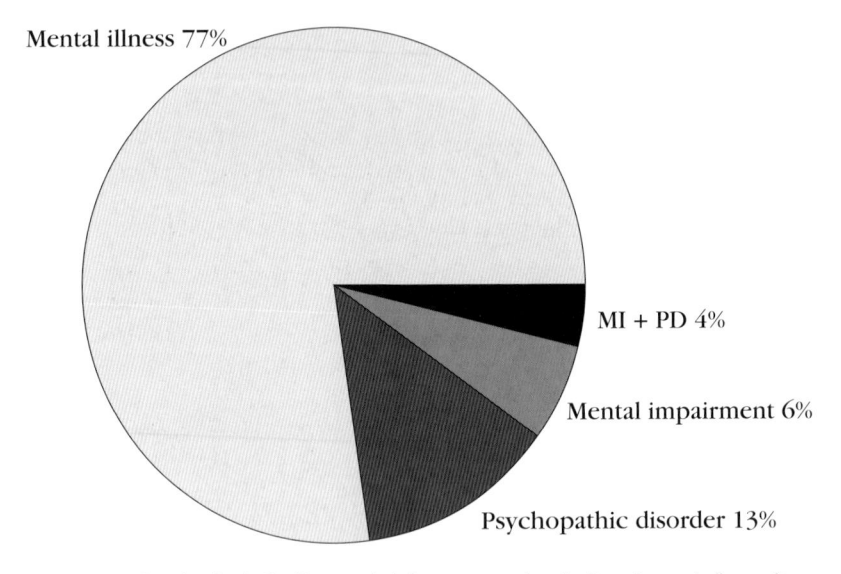

Mental illness 77%

MI + PD 4%

Mental impairment 6%

Psychopathic disorder 13%

* Notes: 'Psychopathic disorder' in this context includes some cases where the diagnosis was actually one of severe personality disorder (psychopathic disorder being one type of personality disorder). 'Mental impairment' is used here, although psychiatrists often used the broader term 'mental handicap'.

In fact, the MHA category and the main diagnosis were the same in most cases, the only notable difference being that, whereas 16 offenders had MI + PD as their main diagnosis, 20 offenders were placed in that MHA category. In those cases (n=24) in which there were either no reports, no diagnosis, or no majority diagnosis, the MHA category was used as a proxy for diagnosis.

Women were twice as likely as men to have a main diagnosis of psychopathic disorder, but markedly less likely to have one of mental illness. Black offenders were significantly more likely to have been diagnosed as mentally ill than white offenders (96% versus 69%). All the Asian offenders were classified as being mentally ill. Only one black offender had a main diagnosis of psychopathic disorder (although two were included in the MI + PD dual category).

---

7   For any case, the principal diagnosis was either that put forward in all the psychiatric reports prepared for court, or that given in a majority of reports (84% of case files included more than one psychiatric report, with an average of three per case).

Demographic information

A full breakdown of demographic information by main diagnostic group is presented in Appendix A.

Sex

The great majority of the sample (88%) were male.

Age

When the restriction orders were imposed, the youngest offender was aged 16 and the oldest 84 with the average age being 31 years. Half of the sample were aged between 21–30 years, and a further quarter between 31–40 years (the average age was 31 years). The variation between the average ages of the different diagnostic groups was statistically significant, although there were no significant difference in age in terms of ethnic group or sex.

Ethnicity

Although the majority of the sample were white (70%), there was a relatively high proportion of black african or black caribbean people in the sample (21%)[8]. The remainder of the sample were either Asian (3%), or from other ethnic groups (5%). Previous studies of patients compulsorily detained under the MHA 1983 (e.g. McGovern and Cope, 1987) have also found the representation of black people to be higher than would be expected from their proportion in the population.

Boast and Chesterman (1995) argue that while any one of such factors as arrest rates, criminal history, psychiatric diagnosis, and the form of admission to mental health services influence the over-representation of black people in secure psychiatric facilities, it is most likely that the over-representation is due to a combination and interaction of a number of complex socio-economic and institutional processes (such as differential diagnosis, the role of stereotypes, and cultural factors underpinning concepts of mental disorder). As this study was not designed specifically to look at ethnic differences, it does not contain explanatory variables of that nature. Nevertheless, some of the ethnic differences revealed by subsequent analysis (e.g. in degree of injury caused, or offending history) might at least partly account for the high proportion of black people in the sample.

---

8   It should be noted that black people made up 21 per cent of the 336 cases where ethnicity was known, but 19 per cent of the total sample; the former figure was used for analysis. The 1991 Census indicated that black people make up about two per cent of the population of England and Wales. An interesting statistic to compare with the figures for restriction orders is that 11 per cent of the prison population were black, as of 30 June 1993 (Prison Statistics, Home Office 1993).

Employment

Only 11 per cent of the sample were in any form of paid employment at the time of their index offence. Many had either never had a job, or had not worked for some time, possibly due to their often extensive psychiatric histories. The only significant difference of note revealed in analysis of employment data by sex, diagnosis and ethnicity, was that offenders in the psychopathic disorder group were significantly more likely to have been employed than those in the other diagnostic groups.

Marital status

Over two-thirds of the sample (68%) were single (and had never been married) when they committed their index offence, with just 13 per cent of offenders either being married or cohabiting. The remainder were either divorced/separated or widowed.

Living arrangements

Appendix A indicates that, at the time of their offence, it was predominantly those in the mental impairment group who were not living in secure, long-term accommodation (a privately owned or rented home), with nearly two-thirds of them living in a hospital, hostel, bed and breakfast establishment, or on the streets[9]. At least some of this group were apparently not capable of living independently. A greater proportion of the total sample (41%) were living alone than with either a current or former partner (14%), or with friends or relatives (30%).

About half of the offences committed by the 39 offenders in the sample who were hospital patients at the time of their index offence were committed in hospital (usually against fellow patients or hospital staff).

Type of index offence

As restriction orders are intended for offenders who pose a risk of serious harm to others, it was not surprising to find that most offences were serious ones which probably would have resulted in substantial periods of imprisonment had the offenders not been dealt with under the MHA 1983.

As Table 1.1 shows, very nearly half of the sample were convicted of manslaughter, attempted murder or GBH, with a further quarter convicted of either arson or a sexual offence.

---

9   Hostels, B&B establishments and no fixed accommodation, constitute the 'other' place of abode category in
     Appendix A.

Table 1.1 Index Offence

Main offence	%	N
Manslaughter	16	58
Attempted murder	3	11
GBH	30	111
Other violence (incl. threats to kill)	11	41
Arson	13	48
Robbery	9	34
Rape or buggery	5	19
Other sexual offences	6	24
Other serious offences*	3	12
Other offences*	4	14

* Notes: 'Other serious offences' comprise aggravated burglary, burglary, abduction, firearms offences and false imprisonment. 'Other offences' include theft, criminal damage and public order offences.

In addition to the main offence, just under a third of the sample (29%, n=109) had been convicted of further subsidiary offences: 21% were convicted of one other offence, six percent of two other offences, and two percent of three or more other offences.

Injury caused

The reported level of injury to victims was examined. While in most cases this provided a simple indication of offence seriousness, some sexual offences where violence had not been used were more difficult to assess. Nonetheless, this analysis showed that 16 per cent (n=59) of the offenders had killed someone[10], 23 per cent (n=85) had caused serious injury (i.e. that which was likely to have required urgent medical attention), and 28 per cent (n=103) caused some other, less serious injury.

In most of the 121 cases where there was no actual injury, the offence either nearly caused serious injury (for example, cases of attempted murder or arson attacks on residential buildings), or the offender behaved in a threatening or aggressive way. In only 13 cases was there no actual or potential injury, or threatening behaviour (for example, those involving arson in empty or non-residential buildings). In some such instances, the offender's suitability for a restriction order appeared to have been inferred from factors other than the nature of the index offence (reflecting that a restriction order is imposed as a consequence of perceived risk rather than harm caused). For example, in one of these cases, a man who had no previous convictions, and whose index offence was a non-residential

---

10   This figure includes one case where a woman was convicted of concealing the birth of a child. The child in question died after being abandoned.

burglary, expressed a series of violent and sadistic fantasies in interviews with psychiatrists. This was sufficient to persuade them that the man presented a very serious threat to the public.

The potential for causing future harm to others among these latter cases was thus usually manifest either in the particular circumstances of the index offence or in disturbing features of the offender's mental disorder. In addition, most had previous convictions for violent or sexual offences, and most had previously been treated compulsorily under the MHA. Nevertheless, there were a few seemingly anomalous cases where, on the evidence available, the risk of future serious harm was not readily apparent. One such example was a man whose index offence was shoplifting (with an additional breach of a probation order). He suffered from chronic schizophrenia, and had a history of non-compliance with treatment and of disruptive (and occasionally aggressive) behaviour while in hospital.

Differences in index offence by sex, diagnostic group and ethnicity

Nearly two-thirds (61%) of women in the sample were convicted of serious violent offences (manslaughter, attempted murder, causing GBH), compared to just under half of the men (47%) and a significantly higher proportion of women were convicted of arson (32% versus 10% of men).

Although offence type varied by sex, the seriousness of the offending behaviour, measured in terms of injury caused, was actually quite similar. A higher proportion of women (23%) killed someone than did men (15%), but men were rather more likely to have caused injury (other than fatal injury) than women (52% versus 39%). Neither of these differences was statistically significant. Of the offenders who caused serious or fatal injuries to others, none of the 124 men offended against their own children, compared to nine (45%) of the 20 women, a strongly significant difference.

The mental illness and the MI + PD groups were not only more likely to have been convicted of manslaughter than the psychopathic disorder or mental impairment groups, but were also more likely to have been convicted of other violent assaults and threats to kill, and robbery. The mentally impaired offenders were more likely to have been convicted of a sexual offence than the other groups, while the psychopathic disorder group were significantly more likely to have been convicted of arson.

Variations between the different diagnostic groups in terms of the harm caused by their offending largely reflected differences in the sorts of offences committed, with mentally ill and MI + PD offenders being more likely to have caused death or serious injury than those diagnosed as psychopathically disordered or mentally impaired.

There were significant differences between black offenders and those from the other ethnic groups in the degree of injury caused by the index offence: 85 per cent (n=61) of black offenders in the sample either killed or caused injury compared to 75 per cent (n=186) of the others. In terms of offence type, black offenders were only slightly more likely (and not significantly so) to have committed an offence of violence or a sexual offence. However, they were less likely to have committed arson or robbery than offenders from other ethnic groups. The latter offences typically did not involve actual injury to others, accounting for the difference in harm caused.

Relationship to victim

A direct victim of the index offence could be identified in 332 cases (89% of the sample). In over half of these cases (53%) the victim was either a partner (or former partner), family member, friend, or acquaintance of the offender. Thirty three per cent of cases involved strangers as the victims, and a further 14 per cent involved someone acting towards the offender in an official capacity (usually a police officer, doctor or nurse).

In the 40 cases where there was no direct victim, the index offence was most commonly arson, although some of these incidents of fire-setting caused substantial property damage (and might, had circumstances been different, have endangered the lives of others).

The nature of the victim was strongly associated with the violence rating of the offence. Thus, the most serious violence was used against those known to the offender: 61 per cent of those who offended against a victim known to them caused either death or serious injury, compared to 23 per cent of those who offended against strangers[11].

The type of offences committed by the mentally impaired and the psychopathically disordered offenders (arson in particular) meant that they were less likely to involve a direct victim. In addition, a quarter of the offences committed by women did not involve a victim, compared to nine per cent of men. However, as indicated previously, when women committed violent offences, they were significantly more likely than men to have their own child as principal victim (27% versus 1%).

Black offenders were more likely than white offenders or those from other ethnic groups to have had a direct victim of their offence, and were more

Previous convictions

Seventy-four per cent of the sample had a criminal history at the time of their index offence (see Appendix C for more details). Two-thirds of these (49% of the total sample) had convictions for a violent or a sexual offence. For those with a criminal record, the average length of time between their first conviction and their index conviction was 12.3 years (sd=8.3), with a range of under one year to 42 years.

Seventy-one per cent (n=125) of offenders whose index offence was a violent one had a previous conviction for violence, while 50 per cent (n=16) of sex offenders had a previous conviction for a sexual offence.

Forty per cent of the sample had served at least one previous custodial sentence, either as an adult or a young offender (including borstal).

The MI + PD group were the most likely to have both a previous conviction of any sort (88%) and one for a sexual or violent offence (63%). The mentally ill were the least likely to have any sort of previous conviction (71%) while mentally impaired offenders, although the most likely to have been convicted of sexual index offence, were the least likely to have a previous conviction for either a sexual or violent offence (38%).

Men were significantly more likely than women to have previous convictions of any sort (77% versus 55%). This difference was particularly marked for violence, where the figures were 50 per cent for men compared with 27 per cent for women. However, women were significantly more likely to have previous convictions for arson.

Black offenders were significantly more likely than those from other ethnic groups to have previous convictions for violent offences (60% versus 43%) and sexual offences (18% versus 10%), which may partially explain their seemingly disproportionate likelihood of receiving a restriction order.

Unprosecuted behaviour

Convictions are usually an undercount of offences committed. In half of the cases in the study there was also some mention (usually in psychiatric reports) of previous violent or otherwise dangerous behaviour, ranging from arson to assaults, which had not been prosecuted. Although allegations of offending behaviour may of course be unfounded, it was nevertheless felt that information about unprosecuted incidents was worth considering. The reports of both the recent Christopher Clunis (Ritchie et al., 1994) and Andrew Robinson (Blom-Cooper et al., 1995) inquiries raised concerns about the failure of agencies to act upon reported violence by the mentally disordered. Such information could also, as 'antecedents', be considered as part of the criteria for imposing a restriction order under section 41 MHA 1983.

One reason for no official action being taken in these incidents seemed to be that they often involved family members or medical staff rather than the general public. There was a significant association between reported dangerous behaviour and having previous convictions for a violent or sexual offence. There were no significant differences, however, in terms of ethnicity, diagnostic group, or type of index offence. Furthermore, despite the difference between the sexes in previous convictions, similar proportions of men and women (approximately half) were reportedly involved in these incidents of unprosecuted harmful behaviour.

Type of hospital

Half the sample were initially admitted to medium secure psychiatric hospitals (usually regional secure units (RSU)) after their restriction order was imposed. Twenty-seven per cent went to the three high security special hospitals, and the remaining 23 per cent went to local hospitals (usually ones with locked wards or interim secure units). Four-fifths of the sample were already in hospital at the time of sentence, having either been remanded, transferred[13], or bailed there, although they were sometimes transferred to a different hospital once the restriction order was imposed.

Significantly more of the psychopathic disorder group went to a special hospital than the other diagnostic groups (60% compared to 20% of the mentally ill, 38% of the mentally impaired and 44% of the MI + PD group). Over half of the mentally ill group went to a RSU/MSU, and about a quarter went to local psychiatric hospitals.

All but eight offenders were in either prison or hospital at some stage during the remand period. Nearly three-quarters of the sample spent time in *both* prison and hospital.

Psychiatric history

Appendix B shows that a majority of the sample had experienced previous contact with psychiatric services. A significantly higher proportion of women (96%) than men (81%) had received psychiatric treatment previously. Nearly three-quarters of the women had been in-patients on two or more previous occasions, compared to just over half of the men.

Just over half the sample were known to have received some form of psychiatric treatment in the six months prior to the index offence, mostly as in-patients, suggesting an immediate history of active mental disorder. It was noted that psychiatric reports sometimes mentioned that a person had either failed to take prescribed medication or attend out-patient appointments.

Age at first in-patient admission varied considerably, the range being 11- to 60-years-old. The average age at first admission was 22.7 years.

Just under two-thirds (65%, n=165) of those who had previously been in-patients had been compulsorily treated before under a section of the 1959 or 1983 MHA – 21% under the criminal provisions, 29 per cent under civil provisions, and 15 per cent under both. Nine offenders had been subject to restriction orders before.

Overall, a significantly greater proportion of those in the mental illness and MI + PD groups had previously been detained under a section of the MHA than those in the psychopathic disorder and mental impairment groups, and were more likely to have been an in-patient before (voluntarily or compulsorily): approximately three-quarters of the mental illness and MI + PD groups had been in-patients, compared to just over half of the psychopathic disorder and mental impairment groups.

---

13   Remands to psychiatric hospital for either reports or treatment are possible under sections 35 and 36 MHA 1983, while remand prisoners can be transferred to hospital under section 48.

Just under half of both men and women had been treated under a section of the MHA before. However, men were much more likely than women previously to have been subject to one of the criminal process sections, while women were slightly more likely than men to have been subject to a civil section. These results are similar to the picture for total admissions under the MHA 1983 during this period (Department of Health, 1995).

There was no difference between black and other offenders in terms of the incidence of any previous psychiatric treatment, although black people were significantly more likely to have spent time as an in-patient under a section of the MHA 1983 or MHA 1959: of those who had previously been in-patients, nearly three-quarters of black offenders had been admitted under a section, compared to three-fifths of those from other ethnic groups. While previous compulsory treatment under the MHA might partly account for their greater likelihood of receiving a restriction order, it also raises further questions about why more black people in the sample had been treated under MHA sections in the past.

The relationship between previous treatment and previous convictions

Having previously received psychiatric treatment and having previous convictions were significantly associated. Seventy-seven per cent of those who had previously been treated had previous convictions and 87 per cent of those with previous convictions had previously been treated. This link could be due partly to the effect of MHA sections such as hospital orders (section 37), remands to hospital (sections 35 and 36), and transfers to hospital (sections 47 and 48), which ensure psychiatric treatment, where necessary, for people involved in criminal proceedings. Nevertheless, even when looking just at the 207 offenders who had not previously been treated under a section of the MHA, there was still a statistically significant connection (although less strong) between previous convictions and previous treatment.

There was a small sub-group of 22 offenders (6% of the sample) who had not had any previous psychiatric treatment, had no previous convictions and had no reported incidents of previous dangerous behaviour. All but three of this group were diagnosed as mentally ill (18 of them having a diagnosis of schizophrenia). The index offence for over a third of this group was manslaughter – a significantly higher proportion than in the sample as a whole. Indeed, nearly three-quarters of this sub-group caused either death or serious injury, compared to two-fifths of the sample as a whole. Even though there was no history of harming others, it seemed that the very serious level of violence the offenders had exhibited on this one occasion was sufficient to mark them as posing a significant risk to others.

At the other end of the spectrum were 66 offenders (18% of the sample) who had two or more previous in-patient admissions, a previous conviction for either a violent or a sexual offence, and had reportedly engaged in dangerous behaviour for which they had not been prosecuted. As with those who had no previous convictions or treatment, a high proportion (86%) of this group were categorised as being mentally ill. However, proportionately fewer (33%) had caused death or serious injury with their index offence than the 'no previous treatment/convictions' group.

Alcohol and drugs

Just under half of the sample (n=179) were described as having regularly either misused alcohol or taken illegal drugs at some stage in the year preceding the index offence (although not necessarily around the actual time of the offence). However, only two per cent of the sample were described in psychiatric reports as suffering from alcohol or drug-induced psychosis.

Men were significantly more likely to have misused alcohol or drugs than women. There were no significant differences between the various diagnostic or ethnic groups.

Discharge from hospital

By the conclusion of the data collection for this part of the project (end of March 1995), 17 per cent of the sample were known to have left hospital. Of these, nearly three-quarters had been conditionally discharged by a Mental Health Review Tribunal (MHRT). Of the remaining 18, four were discharged by the Home Secretary, six were absolutely discharged by a MHRT, four had died, three had absconded[14], and one had been deported to his country of origin. Those discharged (conditionally and absolutely) spent an average of 20 months in hospital, and all but five had been originally diagnosed as mentally ill.

A further two offenders had the imposition of their restriction orders (but not their hospital orders) quashed by the Court of Appeal; it was not known whether they were still in hospital.

Those who were no longer in hospital were significantly less likely to have been described in psychiatric reports as presenting a risk to others (see Chapter 2) than those still in hospital (59% versus 73% respectively), and were less likely (although not significantly so) to have been expressly

---

14   Of the three absconders, two had reoffended and been arrested.

recommended for a restriction order by psychiatrists (32% versus 44%). None of the six offenders absolutely discharged had been expressly recommended for a section 41 order.

Key points

- With only a few exceptions, the offenders in the sample had committed serious offences, nearly a half being convicted of manslaughter, attempted murder, or causing GBH, and a further quarter being convicted of either a sexual offence or arson. The victim was most commonly either an acquaintance, a partner, or other family member of the offende.

- Nearly three-quarters of the sample had a criminal record, a majority of these cases including previous convictions for a sexual or a violent offence.

- Over three-quarters of the sample were diagnosed (and categorised) as mentally ill, and just over a tenth as psychopathically disordered.

- More than four-fifths of the sample had experienced previous psychiatric treatment, just over a half of whom had been treated before under sections of the MHA 1959 or 1983.

- There was a markedly high proportion (one-fifth) of black people in the sample.

2 Assessments of risk and sentencing recommendations

The information in this chapter is drawn from the psychiatric reports prepared for court. Under Section 37 MHA 1983, a court must obtain the written or oral evidence of two registered doctors before imposing a hospital order. In addition, Section 41 stipulates that when imposing a restriction order, the judge must first hear the oral evidence of one of the two doctors who gave evidence on the suitability of the hospital order.

For the purposes of the study, in most cases only full psychiatric reports were considered. The standardised Section 37 forms that doctors recommending such an order have to complete tended just to offer a synopsis of their main report and so these were only analysed in the absence of a full report. Other reports prepared for court, such as the Probation Service's Pre-Sentence Report, were not considered.

In addition to providing the court with information about the existence and nature of an offender's mental disorder, psychiatrists frequently commented in their reports on the degree of risk they thought the offender presented. When they considered the offender to be suffering from a treatable disorder, they also usually made recommendations about how he or she should be dealt with. As there was more than one report in most of the cases, the balance of psychiatric opinion was obtained by looking at the majority view expressed in each case.

Risk assessment

The processes of risk assessment are considered in the data drawn from interviews with psychiatrists, which are featured in Chapter 4. For the purposes of the present analysis, risk assessments in psychiatric reports were categorised in four ways:

(1) cases where a majority of reports agreed the offender was a risk either to the public in general, or to particular individuals (sometimes the victims of the index offence). This category includes cases where the offender was thought likely to pose a risk in the future only in

very particular circumstances, or if his or her mental state deteriorated (e.g., as a result of failing to take medication)[15]

(2) cases where an offender was not considered likely to pose a future threat to others, or was thought likely to harm himself/herself only

(3) cases where there was no majority opinion about the extent of risk the offender presented

(4) other assessments where psychiatrists made inconclusive comments about their assessment of risk or, for example, where they commented on the seriousness of the index offence but not the risk of reoffending.

The relevant risk in question was the risk of serious harm to others. Although the nature of the risk was not always discussed in reports, in the majority of cases the index offence had caused (or nearly caused) serious harm and so the offender's capacity to be dangerous in the future was perhaps taken for granted.

Table 2.1 Psychiatrists' assessments of risk

Majority assessment of risk	%	N
Actual or potential risk to others	70	261
Not a risk to others or risk only to self	6	24
No consensus on risk between psychiatrists	4	14
Other assessments	3	9
No assessment made or no reports	17	64

As Table 2.1 shows, offenders were considered to be a risk to others in 70 per cent of all cases (amounting to 87% of the 299 cases where an explicit opinion on future risk was expressed).

Just six offenders were not described as likely to pose a risk to others in *any* of their psychiatric reports. Nonetheless, their index offences were serious (manslaughter, robbery, indecent assault and arson), and all but one had previous convictions for a violent or a sexual offence.

It appeared that psychiatrists largely took the straightforward view that those offenders who committed the most serious index offences were the most likely to pose a risk to others in the future. Thus three-quarters of those offenders who had caused death or serious injury, or nearly caused serious

---

15 This category combines those whom Walker (1991) has suggested could be defined separately as being 'conditionally', and 'unconditionally', dangerous.

injury, were described as presenting a risk to others, compared to just under two-thirds of those whose index offence had resulted in lesser injury.

Although those with previous convictions for violent or sexual offences were no more likely to have been described as presenting a risk to others than those without such a criminal history, reports of previous unprosecuted violent behaviour were significantly associated with an offender being considered to pose a risk to others.

Possibly because of the association indicated in Chapter 1 between nature of victim and offence seriousness (the victims suffering the most serious harm tended to be those known to the offender), those who had offended against people known to them were more likely to be thought a risk than those who offended against strangers.

There was no statistically significant difference between the main diagnostic groups in terms of risk assessment, but the MI + PD group were the most likely (81%), and the mentally ill group the least likely (68%) to be considered a risk to others.

Less than a third of those offenders who had received time-limited orders were described as presenting a risk to others, compared to nearly three-quarters of those on indefinite orders, a strongly significant difference.

Factors such as levels of previous psychiatric treatment, sex, ethnicity, previous drug or alcohol misuse, or age when sentenced, were not significantly associated with the likelihood of being described as presenting a risk to others (although black people were both more likely than other offenders to be described as posing a risk to others, and to be recommended for either a restricted hospital order or an unrestricted one in conditions of high security).

There is a possibility that in some cases psychiatrists did not make (or note) an explicit assessment that an offender posed a risk, but intimated as much by recommending them for a restriction order. Nevertheless, there were 91 offenders for whom there was no majority assessment of being a risk to others or no majority recommendation for a restriction order. While equally likely to have previous convictions for a serious offence, this group tended to have been charged with less serious index offences than the remainder of the sample. Interestingly, nearly a quarter of the group had robbery as their index offence compared to just five per cent of the rest of the sample.

Recommendations

The sentencing recommendations in the psychiatric reports were also examined in order to look at how far restriction orders were recommended by doctors and to what extent they were imposed in cases without such a recommendation. Although section 41 makes it clear that the decision to impose a restriction order is solely the judge's, and that he or she can do so even in the face of opposition from psychiatrists, the Court of Appeal in *R v Birch* (1990) emphasised that the doctors' opinions should be an important consideration in the court's conclusion that a restriction order is necessary.

Table 2.2 shows that a restriction order was expressly recommended by a majority of psychiatric reports in 41 per cent of cases, and an unrestricted hospital order in a further 33 per cent.

Table 2.2 Psychiatrists' recommendations

Majority recommendation	%	N
Restriction Order	41	154
Hospital order	33	124
Other psychiatric treatment	1	2
No recommendation for psychiatric treatment	2	9
No majority recommendation	17	65
No recommendation made or no reports	5	18

Of the 154 restriction order recommendations, in 81 cases the recommendations were made primarily because of the risk posed by the offender. In another 13 cases, the main reason given for a restriction order recommendation was the need to provide long-term supervised treatment for the offender, both in and out of hospital. However, nine of these 13 offenders were also assessed in the reports as posing a risk to others. In most of the remaining 55 cases a mix of reasons (usually a combination of the need for security and supervision) was given.

The 124 unrestricted hospital order recommendations included just four cases (1% of the sample) where the majority of reports recommended a hospital order but expressly opposed the addition of a restriction order. In 11 cases the main recommendation was for a hospital order but with the proviso that the court might wish to consider imposing a restriction order, while in a further seven cases the majority recommendation was for a hospital order in conditions of maximum security. These latter 18 cases therefore are ones where the doctors involved were seemingly not opposed to the imposition of a restriction order, but may have felt that they should not actually recommend one in their report. Overall, just over half of those offenders recommended for unrestricted hospital orders (55%) were assessed in a majority of reports as being likely to present a risk to others.

The main distinguishing feature of those expressly recommended for restriction orders, compared to those who were not was the degree of harm caused by the index offence: not surprisingly, restriction orders were recommended significantly more often when the index offence was relatively more serious. For example, restriction orders were recommended for well over half of those convicted of manslaughter, but for only 13 per cent of those convicted of robbery.

Other than this, there was little to distinguish the two groups. While a close relationship was expected between risk assessments and recommendations, only just over half of those who were assessed as posing a risk to others were recommended for a restriction order in their psychiatric reports. The fact that psychiatrists thought that the majority of offenders posed a risk to others, but only expressly recommended restriction orders in a minority of cases suggests that they often decided to leave the consideration solely to the judge. However, it is not known of course whether some psychiatrists concerned might have expanded upon their reports when questioned in court as to the appropriateness of a restriction order being imposed.

The MI + PD group were the most likely to have been recommended for a restriction order (56%), followed by the psychopathically disordered (48%), the mentally ill (40%), and lastly the mentally impaired (29%).

A higher proportion of women than men were recommended for restriction orders (50% versus 40%) and a lower proportion recommended for hospital orders (23% versus 35%). Black offenders were more likely to be recommended for restriction orders than were white and Asian offenders (49% versus 39% and 36% respectively). None of these differences were statistically significant, however.

While constructing a majority recommendation for each case simplified analysis considerably and allowed us to look at the balance of opinion, this approach is rather artificial – not least because the earlier reports may have only been concerned with whether the defendant was suitable for either a transfer or a remand to hospital. Because of this, further analysis was undertaken on the *latest* (and thus most up-to-date) psychiatric report in each case.

This analysis showed that of the 354 cases where there was a recommendation as to final disposal made by a psychiatrist, the *latest* recommendation in 201 cases (57%) supported the imposition of a section 41 order. An additional 30 (8%) of the latest recommendations mentioned the imposition of a section 41 order as a possibility, and in 11 (3%) cases a section 37 order was recommended but conditions of high or maximum security were stipulated.

Furthermore, in two-thirds (n=43) of the 65 reports where there was no majority recommendation, the latest psychiatric report recommended a restriction order, whereas an unrestricted hospital order was recommended in just 20 cases.

There was evidence on file of active disagreement between psychiatrists in only 31 cases (8% of the total sample) about either diagnosis (including whether an offender was really mentally disordered or not), the level of risk posed by an offender, or the appropriate disposal.

Judicial comments

In nine cases there was evidence of the judge having made (mainly adverse) comments on psychiatric recommendations. Usually, the judge wished to pass a restriction order but the psychiatrists involved in the case either did not feel that a restriction order was warranted, or would not offer a bed to the offender in question. In 14 cases (including one case where the judge also commented upon the psychiatric recommendations) there was evidence on file of the judge commenting upon the risk posed by the offender (generally in the form of extracts from the judge's summing up). Not surprisingly, in all of these cases the judge described the offender in question as presenting a risk to others. In the great majority of cases, however, there was no information contained in the files as to the judge's view of the risk posed by the offender or the psychiatrists' recommendations.

Key points

- Seventy per cent of the sample were described by a majority of psychiatric reports as being likely to pose a risk to others. Those offenders who had committed the most serious index offences were the most likely to be considered a risk.

- Just two-fifths of the sample were expressly recommended for restriction orders. However, this may reflect the fact that some psychiatrists felt that it was not their responsibility to recommend section 41 orders in their reports. In the *latest* report in each case, the proportion of the sample recommended for a restriction order was nearly three-fifths.

- Again, seriousness of the index offence appeared to be the factor most strongly associated with a recommendation for a restriction order.

- Of the diagnostic groups, MI + PD offenders were both the most likely to be considered a risk to others, and the most likely to be recommended by doctors for a restriction order.

3. Comparison with offenders receiving unrestricted hospital orders

In order to compare those offenders who received restriction orders with those who were given unrestricted hospital orders in the same period, the Home Office Offenders Index (OI) was used to draw a sample of offenders who received unrestricted Section 37 hospital orders in 1992 and 1993 for a non-summary offence. Any offender who also had a restriction order imposed during those years was excluded. This gave a total of 984 offenders in the Section 37 control group[16]. Their characteristics were then compared with similar data, also drawn from the Offenders Index, for the main sample of restricted offenders (the sample group). There was some loss of data because full Offenders Index details were only available for 302 (81%) of the main sample[17].

Demographic data

The control and sample groups were compared for: sex; age at index conviction; and age at first conviction. None of these comparisons revealed any statistically significant difference between the groups. For example, nearly 90 per cent of both groups were male. Both groups were on average about 30-years-old when convicted of their index offence (the sample group were on average slightly older), and both on average around 20-years-old when first convicted (the sample group were on average slightly younger). However, the variations between the samples, although slight, meant that those in the sample group with previous convictions had, on average, a significantly longer offending history by the time of their index conviction than their control group counterparts – 12.0 years compared to 10.5 years.

---

16 These 984 offenders represent 91 per cent of those who received unrestricted hospital orders for non-summary offences in 1992 and 1993 (according to Home Office Criminal Statistics).

17 This resulted in some small variations from the data collected from MHU files, particularly for age at first conviction, which was 18.5 years according to the file data, and 19.2 years according to OI data. However, this difference may be due less to sample differences and more to the fact that the OI records only non-summary offence convictions starting in 1963, whereas criminal records information held in the MHU files would typically show all previous conviction information, irrespective of type of offence or date of conviction.

Index offence

Differences between the two groups were much more marked in respect of the nature of index offence, as Table 3.1 indicates. The only difference of any note between the sample group here and that discussed in Chapter one (where the data was drawn from MHU files rather than from the OI) was that the proportion of the latter convicted of 'Other violence' was nine per cent, compared to the 12 per cent shown for this group.

Table 3.1 Comparison of index offences

Index offence	s37 control group %	N	s37/41 sample %	N
Manslaughter	1	13	16	47
Serious violence	13	132	34	104
Other violence	23	227	12	35
Rape/buggery	2	16	5	16
Other sexual offences	7	70	6	18
Robbery	6	62	8	24
Arson	9	89	12	37
Burglary	10	90	1	4
Theft	13	124	1	3
Criminal damage	7	73	1	1
Public order	6	57	2	7
Other	3	31	2	6
	N=984		N=302	

Considerably more of the sample group had been convicted of manslaughter and serious violence (attempted murder and GBH) than had the control group – 50 per cent versus 14 per cent.

Comparing the two groups over offences most likely to have caused (or with the potential to cause) harm to others (violence against the person, robbery, sexual offences and arson) showed that 93 per cent of the sample group had committed such an index offence, compared to 62 per cent of the control group.

Conversely, significantly more of the control group had been convicted of offences against property (excluding arson and robbery) – 30 per cent versus three per cent – or public order – six per cent versus two per cent – than had the sample group.

Previous convictions

Table 3.2 compares information on previous convictions and court disposals for the sample and control groups.

Table 3.2 Comparison of criminal history information

	s37 control group	s37/41 sample
percentage with any type of previous conviction	67%	71%
percentage with previous conviction for a violent offence	37%	46%
percentage with a previous conviction for a sexual offence	6%	8%
percentage previously given a custodial sentence	35%	35%
percentage previously given a hospital order (with or without s41)	14%	16%
percentage previously given any type of mental health disposal at court	18%	20%

Of the differences shown above, the only one that was statistically significant was the variation in previous convictions for violent offences.

However, the differences between the two groups in terms of any association between type of past and index offences was significant. Twenty-eight per cent of those in the sample group whose index conviction was for a violent offence had previously been convicted of violence, compared to just 15 per cent of the control group with a violent index offence. Overall, 47 per cent of the sample group who were convicted of either a violent offence, a sexual offence, or arson, also had previous convictions for at least one of those types of offence compared to 25 per cent of the control group.

Also statistically significant was the difference in the average number of previous convictions: of those with previous convictions, offenders in the sample group had been convicted over seven times, compared to just over six times for those in the control group.

There was no significant difference between the two groups in terms of previous imprisonment: just over a third (35%) of either group had received at least one previous custodial sentence. Nor was there any marked difference in respect of previous court mental health disposals generally, or previous hospital/restriction orders specifically the figures for the sample group being 20 per cent and 16 per cent respectively, compared to 18% and 14% respectively for the control group.

For those members of either group who had *no* previous convictions (and thus fewer 'antecedents' for consideration), nearly two-thirds (58%) of those who received restriction orders had been convicted of serious violence (as defined above), compared to just one-fifth (18%) of those given an unrestricted Section 37 order. Meanwhile, just under a quarter (23%) of the control group who did not have a criminal record had been convicted of either theft, public order or criminal damage, compared with none of their sample group counterparts.

Discussion

Important variables that would be expected to be factors in the degree of risk posed by a mentally disordered offender, such as those relating to diagnosis, psychiatric history, and the particular circumstances of the index offence, were not available for the purposes of this comparison. Nevertheless, the data in the preceding chapters, as well as the wording of Section 41 itself, make it clear that seriousness of index offence and criminal history will be significant considerations in the assessment of risk and thus the decision to impose a restriction order. Consequently, the differences found here between the control and sample groups could be regarded as robust indicators of whether a Section 37, or a Section 37/41, order was imposed. However, the fact that some of the control group had committed serious index offences, while some of the sample group had committed relatively less serious ones, highlights the fact that restriction orders are imposed on basis of likely future risk, and not harm already caused (as affirmed by the Court of Appeal in *R v Courtney*, 1988).

Key points

- The sample group were more likely to have been convicted of offences of serious violence, and other serious offences like rape and arson. Conversely the control group were more likely to have been convicted of property offences (excluding arson).

- The sample group were significantly more likely to have a previous conviction for a violent offence.

- The two groups were fairly similar in terms of: age at index conviction; age at first conviction; previous convictions for any type of offence; and levels of previous imprisonment and court mental health disposals.

4 Interviews with judges and psychiatrists

To complement the data extracted from MHU files, semi-structured interviews were carried out with small samples of judges and psychiatrists to seek their views on issues relating to the use of restriction orders.

Seven senior judges at Crown Court centres in major cities in England and Wales were interviewed, as were six forensic psychiatrists (drawn from hospitals of differing levels of security). Although the number of interviews was thus quite small, both the judges and psychiatrists were selected for interview on the basis of their experience in dealing with restriction order cases. The questions were mainly about the process of imposing restriction orders, although some questions relating to discharge from hospital were included. The views they expressed were, of course, personal ones and not necessarily representative of the two professions as a whole.

Aims of restriction orders

Both the judges and the psychiatrists thought that the primary aim of a restriction order was to protect the public, as the MHA 1983 specifies. However, the two groups differed in their views as to how the order achieved this aim.

The judges tended to say that the restriction order aimed to protect the public by securely detaining the patient and restricting their discharge until they were adjudged safe to be released. Some of the judges likened restriction orders to 'longer than normal' sentences under Section 2(2)(b) of the Criminal Justice Act 1991, saying that both provisions aimed to put dangerous offenders out of circulation.

Community supervision was seen by judges as an important feature of the restriction order, though subordinate to ensuring secure detention with restrictions on discharge from hospital. One judge thought that restriction orders had an important demonstrative role, saying: "by making a restriction order you are allaying public anxiety about the presence of that defendant in the community, and the risk of him repeating the offence for which he has been convicted".

Some judges identified benefit to the patient as being a feature of the restriction order, in that the order would guarantee them treatment, probably over a prolonged period, but principally their view was that the therapeutic element was covered by the hospital order and that the restriction order was solely concerned with protecting the public.

The psychiatrists also stressed the paramount importance of public safety and felt the order protected the public by placing added safeguards on psychiatric practice in the case of dangerous mentally disordered offenders. One psychiatrist said the restriction order was an acknowledgement that "psychiatrists should not be the sole guardians of public safety" in these type of cases. However, the psychiatrists thought that the restriction order worked to protect the public not only by ensuring that a doctor's ability to control and discharge his or her own patient was restricted and monitored externally, but also crucially by providing (through the conditional discharge system) an effective framework to ensure longer-term treatment and supervision in the community.

Like the judges, the psychiatrists also said that restriction orders could be of benefit to the patient by ensuring thorough treatment and thus hopefully preventing them from reoffending. Through the conditional discharge system, patients could also be enabled to stay well and at liberty. One psychiatrist contrasted this with his experience of dangerous patients held on Section 3 of the MHA 1983, who because of concerns about the risk they posed and the (then) absence of any effective community supervision following discharge[18], could not be safely released from hospital.

Reasons for imposing or recommending restriction orders

There was a close correspondence between the perceived aims of restriction orders, and reasons given by the interviewees for either imposing or recommending them.

The judges emphasised that in such cases they followed the MHA guidelines and Court of Appeal guidance laid down in cases such as *R v Birch* (1990), and *R v Gardiner* (1967). Firstly, they would look to see if the defendant fulfilled the necessary criteria for the imposition of a Section 37 order. Then, if the defendant appeared additionally to pose a risk of serious harm to others, the judges would consider adding a Section 41 order. Traditional sentencing aims were said to play no part in the decision to impose a restriction order, nor did notions of a tariff sentence for the offence in question.

18 New arrangements for post-discharge care and supervision of psychiatric patients have been introduced by the supervised discharge provisions of the Mental Health (Patients in the Community) Act 1995, which came into force on 1 April 1996.

The level of risk posed by the offender was the key issue. While the type of index offence was obviously an important factor in determining that risk, the judges stressed that it was the circumstances surrounding the offence, rather than just the nature of the charge, that was crucial.

Some of the judges were of the opinion that if the case was serious enough to have come to the Crown Court and the defendant was sufficiently disordered to warrant a hospital order, then it would be rare not to add a restriction order. One judge thought that there was a presumption in such cases that a Section 41 order would be appropriate. Another judge said that defendants on serious charges invariably seemed to get restriction orders but thought this indicated that some judges possibly made restriction orders a little too readily.

One judge said that he had recently presided over a case where the psychiatrists involved had recommended a restriction order so as to ensure the patient's compliance with medication once released. He had told psychiatrists that this was not a statutory consideration, and so while he would make the order, he would be ignoring that as a reason for doing so.

Like the judges, the psychiatrists said that the principal reason for them recommending a restriction order would be the degree of risk posed by the offender. For a restriction order to be considered, in most cases they thought that the offender would have to have committed a serious or *potentially* serious offence, although it was again emphasised that the nature of the offence was just one among a number of factors to be considered.

History of non-compliance with previous treatment (and persistent subsequent relapses) was also mentioned in some interviews as a factor in favour of a restriction order, as was a patient's lack of insight into their disorder. Although it was emphasised that these factors would only usually be of concern if they increased the level of risk, it was suggested that restriction orders might occasionally be recommended by some doctors to deal with the problem of non-compliance and relapses *per se*.

Where the psychiatrists really differed from the judges was in their view that the long-term supervision afforded by the conditional discharge system was a (if not, the) major advantage to a restriction order. Although only two of the psychiatrists said explicitly that they would recommend a restriction order so as to secure eventual treatment under a conditional discharge, all of the psychiatrists stressed that for them the real value of the restriction order lay in the conditional discharge system (one doctor remarked that the length of time it usually takes to get a restricted patient discharged from hospital made recommending a restriction order solely to ensure community supervision prohibitive). A restriction order was described as making little significant difference to a patient's management or care while in hospital, but becoming crucially important following discharge from hospital, where the real difficulty in terms of controlling risk was seen to lie.

The psychiatrists' comments reflected their longer-term view of restriction order cases beyond detention in hospital. As one said: "one can keep any patient safe in hospital under medication forever. Sooner or later, however, one has to release them because they're well, or the MHRT will release them because they are well".

Some of the psychiatrists' opinions of the conditional discharge system's value were motivated by perceived deficiencies in present mental health law. Conditional discharge under the Section 41 order was felt to be the only way of then ensuring good quality community care.

The roles of judges and psychiatrists in imposing restriction orders

Both psychiatrists and judges were asked how they perceived their own and each other's role in the process of imposing restriction orders.

Judges were very clear that the power and responsibility to impose restriction orders lay solely with them as part of their general duty to protect the public. However, they commented that Section 41 obliged them to seek the advice of at least one psychiatrist on the suitability of a restriction order, in addition to the psychiatrists' principal role in establishing the clinical need for a hospital order. Psychiatric advice as to whether any restriction order should be time-limited or not was seen as particularly important. The judges stressed that they would give very careful consideration to any recommendation by a psychiatrist for a restriction order, and in practice most of them felt it would be unusual not to follow it. Some added that they thought it rare for a psychiatrist expressly to oppose the imposition of a restriction order.

When asked if they would only consider a restriction order if mentioned in a psychiatric report, the judges said that they would not, with most adding that they thought it quite readily apparent when a restriction order was required.

The judges tended to say that the credence they gave to psychiatric evidence depended to a certain extent upon their perceptions of the psychiatrists in question, the evidence of some doctors being treated with a degree of scepticism. One judge said that his mistrust had arisen from psychiatrists who "do not look realistically enough at dangers to the public". By and large, however, the judges interviewed seemed satisfied with the psychiatric evidence they received, probably because they tended to see the same psychiatrists regularly and so had developed a rapport with them.

Most of the psychiatrists said that they would recommend a restriction order in their report if they felt one was needed, seeing it as part of their job as forensic psychiatrists to do so. One of them added, "if you don't raise the question of a restriction order it leaves it open to the judge to raise that question perhaps in a less informed way". Another commented, however, that some of his older colleagues were loathe even to mention a restriction order, seeing this as part of sentencing and thus the judge's job. One psychiatrist said that he would *not* expressly recommend a restriction order in a report, but would only mention it as a possibility for the court to decide upon (although he said that he would give an opinion on suitability if questioned in court).

The psychiatrists' comments on judicial knowledge of employing restriction orders tended to vary, depending on their personal experience. Mostly, however, they were impressed with the way judges handled restriction order cases. The psychiatrists saw the judges' role as being to take a 'common sense' view of public safety. As one put it, judges, thanks to their legal training, were "capable of taking a very balanced view of all the evidence in a way in which psychiatrists can't".

The importance of the draconian power of a restriction order only being imposed with judicial authority, and marked by a conviction, was also stressed by some of the psychiatrists. Judges could thus provide a check upon the capacity of overly-liberal or overly-cautious psychiatrists to discharge or detain patients inappropriately.

Some of the psychiatrists, however, did feel that their rather different, longer-term view of the use of restriction orders could perhaps lead to some disagreements or misunderstanding with judges who principally saw the restriction order as a means of removing a dangerous offender from circulation.

Finally, in view of recent public anxiety about dangerous mentally disordered offenders, some psychiatrists expressed concern that judges might increasingly impose life sentences in serious cases involving mentally disordered defendants, rather than restriction orders, because of their concerns about inappropriate discharges, or even impose lengthy time-limited restriction orders (although of course a patient can still be conditionally discharged on a time-limited order). However, these fears were not borne out in the judges' comments.

Risk assessment

Section 41 of the MHA 1983 makes it very clear that risk is the key issue in the imposition of a restriction order, and this was reflected in the interviewees' comments.

While some respondents stressed that, broadly speaking, the more serious the index offence, the more likely an offender would be considered dangerous, they reiterated that of course the type of offence was not the key consideration. Consequently, cases where the harm caused was perhaps *potentially* rather than *actually* serious could well qualify for a restriction order. One of the psychiatrists gave an example of a man whose index offence was criminal damage, but the damage in question had been breaking the window of a mortuary in an attempt to enter and then engage in necrophilia. If access to corpses in this way was not possible, he was prepared to kill. So although on paper the index offence was only criminal damage, the man was considered to be highly dangerous and was given a restriction order.

Judges emphasised that they followed the statute and case law (particularly Lord Justice Mustill's guidance in *R v Birch*) when assessing risk, focusing in particular upon the circumstances of the index offence and the defendant's antecedents (as Section 41 stipulates). The risk in question was that presented by the offender now and in the immediate future, not in years to come. The term 'antecedents' was construed by the judges to include not just previous convictions, but also accounts of previous unprosecuted dangerous behaviour made in psychiatric reports (subject to any objection by defence counsel), and some said that evidence of the failure of previous treatment might also be significant. A history of violence would cause particular concern, especially if it appeared that the violence was escalating in seriousness.

While the judges thought psychiatrists' advice on risk was important (they also welcomed any assessment by the Probation Service included in Pre-Sentence Reports), overall they did not seem to feel that risk assessment in these cases caused them any particular difficulties. Many of them said that risk assessment was a daily part of their job, and in any case it was usually clear to them whether or not a restriction order was likely to be required. Nevertheless, one judge did say that cases involving a very serious offence (such as manslaughter), where the offender had no previous convictions and the offence appeared to be a 'one-off', made the assessment of risk difficult.

The psychiatrists tended to give a more detailed account of what they saw as the painstaking process of risk assessment and also focused more upon the future management of risk, which they saw as their responsibility in the longer term. One psychiatrist said that he thought that doctors had the opportunity to do a more thorough risk assessment before sentencing than did judges. While the judges naturally concentrated upon the criminological risk factors (index offence, previous convictions), the psychiatrists spent much time discussing the clinical issues involved in risk – this of course being the area on which judges particularly expected advice.

Past behaviour was seen as usually the best guide to future behaviour, but respondents stressed that situational circumstances could also have an important bearing on risk by interacting with innate risk factors. The degree of control over 'situational risk' that the conditional discharge system provided was one reason for its popularity among the psychiatrists interviewed. Commenting on the difference between assessing risk following the index offence and assessing risk before discharge from hospital, one psychiatrist remarked: "it's very easy to say that someone is dangerous in the immediate aftermath [of an offence], but to turn round in five years time and say that this man is no longer dangerous is far harder to prove".

Reference was frequently made by the psychiatrists to the predictability of dangerous behaviour: if harmful behaviour was predictable, then it was more susceptible to management and thus less of a risk. Consequently, unprovoked attacks on strangers, even though less common than attacks on family or medical staff, were often more worrying as they were less predictable and so less manageable.

Unlike the judges, some of the psychiatrists thought it often less evident what behaviour did or did not constitute risk of serious harm. There were cases where the offender was clearly dangerous, and cases where the offender clearly was not dangerous, but a large area of uncertainty in between. One psychiatrist, discussing the imposition of restriction orders in cases where the index offence had not appeared particularly serious, suggested: "If you see someone who has been put on a restriction order after conviction for common assault, it is more likely that it is going to be persistent relapses that are being dealt with". Equally, it was said that if the index offence was serious but there was thought to be no (or virtually no) chance of repetition, a restriction order might not be necessary.

Views on mental disorder

Both groups of interviewees were asked about the suitability of restriction orders for people suffering from different types of mental disorder.

Understandably, the judges had far less than the doctors to say on the topic. One judge said that it was not his place to have an opinion on mental disorder. Generally, the attitude of the judges was that if the defendant came within the terms of the MHA 1983, then he/she was potentially eligible for a hospital order. As one judge succinctly put it: "if he's [the defendant] really ill, then he's a sick man and should be treated".

Some judges remarked that doctors rarely seemed to recommend restriction orders for psychopathic disorder (PD) patients nowadays, but thought that some psychopaths could cause significant problems, and in some cases might be better suited to prison rather than hospital.

The psychiatrists were split between the view that restriction orders were appropriate for all types of disorder, and the view that, except in rare cases, the restriction order was not suitable for patients with psychopathic personality disorder (although some of those subscribing to the latter opinion conceded that it might be suitable for patients suffering from other types of personality disorder). Overall, the psychiatrists thought the restriction order model best suited mentally ill patients, the conditional discharge system in particular being well suited to treating them and maintaining their stability.

The reservations about PD largely appeared to arise out of psychiatrists' fears of having to care for PD patients who proved uncooperative with treatment while in hospital and then almost impossible to supervise afterwards. Such comments of course acknowledged that the problem lay not just with the nature of PD, but also with the limited availability of services to treat and manage PD successfully. Most PD patients were seen as needing longer-term treatment than medium secure facilities could provide and, in any case, it was unlikely a serious offender with PD would be admitted directly to a RSU. So, as one doctor put it: "treatment for serious offenders with psychopathic disorder is either to go to a maximum secure hospital or to receive a prison term".

Most of the psychiatrists mentioned that the power to add a 'hospital direction' order to a prison sentence, commonly known as the 'hybrid order'[19] (originally proposed by the Department of Health and Home Office Working Group on Psychopathic Disorder, 1994) was worthy of serious consideration for PD patients.

A view expressed by some of the psychiatrists was that the public, and possibly judges, often had a misconception of the nature of some mental illnesses (particularly schizophrenia), seeing them as conditions like pneumonia, in that they could be treated decisively and then the patient

---

19   The 'hospital and limitation directions' (as they are called) have now been enacted in sections 46-49 of the Crime (Sentences) Act 1997. The Home Office consultation paper, "Mentally disordered offenders: sentencing and discharge arrangements" (1996) that preceded the Act suggested that the order could apply to patients suffering from all types of disorder defined by the MHA, and not just psychopathic disorder. However, the Act restricts the order just to those offenders suffering from the latter.

would be well again. In contrast, the psychiatrists thought a more accurate medical analogy would be diabetes, where the sufferer is likely to require long-term treatment, and while he or she might enjoy periods of remission, is unlikely ever to be totally cured.

The process of discharge from hospital

While acknowledging the advantages of the conditional discharge system, overall the judges' comments made it clear that they thought the process of discharge from hospital was not their concern or responsibility: "it's not a judicial act by the sentencing court', said one. They said that they had, and had to have, faith in subsequent decision-makers and that any doubts that a judge might have about release could not possibly affect his or her decision to impose such an order. One judge stressed that it was his job to decide on the basis of the evidence in front of him and not on the basis of his opinions. Another commented that once the order had been passed, subject to appeal, that was the end of his association with the case.

Because of their lack of long-term association with restriction order cases, and their absence of involvement with the discharge process, judges did not tend to hold any strong views on the roles of the MHRTs and the Home Office. Some said they liked the fact that MHRTs for restricted cases would be chaired by a judge, and thought that the tribunals might prevent the sort of very lengthy detention for relatively minor offences that they believed sometimes used to occur. The judges were aware of Home Office involvement in, and responsibility for, restricted cases, but generally had little to add to this, although one judge said that he understood the political pressures that made the Home Office act cautiously (as he saw it) in these type of cases.

The psychiatrists were very positive about discharge from hospital under a restriction order. As one doctor said: "it's a model of how it [discharge] should be done.....Really, there isn't an issue about [discharging] patients on restriction orders". It was felt that discharges should be conditional, to allow effective treatment and supervision in the community. One view expressed was that an absolute discharge within a relatively short time of the restriction order being imposed indicated that the restriction order had been employed inappropriately: "if you [the RMO] are recommending absolute discharge, it is often tantamount to saying that there has been a mistake in imposing a Section 41 in this case".

The psychiatrists thought that, generally, the MHRT process was a good one, lending necessary checks and balances to the restriction order system by providing patients with a legal right to review of their detention. Some of the psychiatrists interviewed thought that MHRTs should have the power to direct transfer between hospitals. Nonetheless, criticisms of the MHRT system were expressed. Tribunals were branded as often being excessively legalistic and their sometimes adversarial nature was seen as being potentially anti-therapeutic.

The psychiatrists were mostly (although not wholly) positive about Home Office involvement. They welcomed being able to share the responsibility of looking after dangerous offenders with the Home Office who, as one doctor put it, "act like an external audit". Some of the psychiatrists remarked that the MHU's collective experience probably outweighed that of individual doctors and that this provided an overview that the clinical team might not have. However, the perceived political aspects of Home Office decisions frustrated the doctors (one example given was a blanket ruling regarding leave for all special hospital patients which arose from an incident at one of the special hospitals). So too did the delays in making decisions or responding to requests, although it was acknowledged that these were generally decisions that should not be rushed. Many of the doctors said that it would be useful if the Home Office could have more direct involvement in cases, but said that they recognised the workload pressures that probably made this impossible.

Advantages and disadvantages of restriction orders

Protecting the public, by ensuring the detention and treatment (usually for an indefinite period) of those mentally disordered offenders thought dangerous, was the principal advantage of restriction order as far as the judges were concerned. They also said that Section 41, and the attendant case law, was clear and unambiguous, and relatively easy for judges to apply. They saw Section 41 as an essential order and none of them could think of any obvious improvements that could be made to the Section.

The psychiatrists tended to see the main advantage of restriction orders as being the conditional discharge system, which ensured compulsory community supervision (in turn lowering the risk of future offending). Restriction orders were thus seen as ensuring thorough and high-quality treatment for patients which they might not receive otherwise. Another significant advantage was that a restriction order meant that responsibility for the management and decision-making in relation to a potentially dangerous patient was shared with others. Some thought that a restriction order marked the severity of the offence in question, which would make future carers and decision-makers take notice. It was also suggested that restriction orders went down well with judges, public and victims (or victims' families).

When asked about disadvantages, some of the judges said that they were occasionally troubled about the issue of proportionality in these cases, where a person might be detained for very lengthy periods on the basis of what they might do rather than what they had done.

One judge said that he thought the adversarial system was not well suited to the process of imposing restriction orders, but none of the other judges saw this as a difficulty. A more common problem for the court was identified as being non-disclosure of psychiatric reports.

Judges also mentioned some difficulties with the mechanics of imposing restriction orders, such as the lack of available secure beds and the numerous adjournments that were often necessary where a restriction order was to be imposed.

Some of the disadvantages mentioned by the psychiatrists were the converse of the advantages. For example, while they recognised that a restriction order prevented doctors from discharging patients too early, they felt that restriction orders constrained their ability to act freely. Furthermore, while Home Office involvement generally reassured psychiatrists, the associated delays in dealing with an external body were seen as not only frustrating, but also possibly anti-therapeutic as patients might become agitated at missing opportunities and their disorder could worsen again.

Becoming responsible for unco-operative PD patients was highlighted by the psychiatrists as being a particularly acute problem. The difficulty of having to supervise patients they would not have recommended for discharge themselves was also mentioned. It was stressed that because of the draconian powers of restriction orders, and the potential repercussions in terms of the patient being 'labelled' as a restricted offender and undergoing possibly lengthy detention, such orders should only be imposed carefully and cautiously.

A few of the psychiatrists mentioned occasional problems with recall to hospital. In particular, they noted that the Home Office had sometimes recalled patients against their advice and that the very fear of recall led to some patients not being totally open with their supervisors about their problems.

Finally, concern was expressed that some psychiatrists had insufficient knowledge, not just of the use of restriction orders, but also of issues surrounding offending and risk assessment generally.

Key points

- Both judges and psychiatrists seemed keenly aware of their duty to protect the public, and the restriction order was seen by both groups as a very valuable way of dealing with a difficult and dangerous group of offenders. Indeed, most of the disadvantages mentioned by the respondents tended to arise from problems with the operation of restriction orders rather than the principles underlying them.

- Although the judges and the psychiatrists seemed broadly in agreement and generally thought their working relationships in this area functioned well, their priorities were somewhat different, reflecting their different roles. Psychiatrists placed emphasis on the long-term treatment and supervision that was often necessary in these cases; while the judges' primary concern was that dangerous offenders should be out of circulation. However, it was generally agreed that the restriction order could serve both aims.

Section two:
A follow-up of discharged restricted patients

5 Description of the sample

It was said by some of the psychiatrists interviewed in the first part of the study that the value of a restriction order only really emerged once a restricted patient[20] had been discharged from hospital – a reference to the supervision provided by the conditional discharge system (for a detailed discussion, see Dell and Grounds, 1995). Furthermore, while a restricted patient will only usually be discharged if it is considered safe to do so, the actual degree of risk posed by the patient and the capacity of the framework provided by the restriction order to manage and control that risk can only truly be tested following the patient's release from hospital.

This Section of the report focuses on those 391 restricted patients[21] who were first discharged from hospital in the years 1987 to 1990. Of these 391, 370 (95%) were conditionally discharged and 21 were absolutely discharged straight from hospital. The conditionally discharged patients were followed up either until they were absolutely discharged, or until the end of December 1994 (whichever was sooner, although any reconvictions occurring up until the end of 1994 were counted). In common with most follow-up studies of discharged psychiatric patients, the study focused on reconvictions and readmission to hospital (as represented by recall to hospital under Section 42(3) MHA 1983), although information was also collected on other aspects of patients' circumstances following discharge.

As there was no other information available on them, the 21 patients absolutely discharged straight from hospital were only followed-up in terms of reconvictions.

First, however, this chapter presents background information about the characteristics of the members of the sample at the time that their restriction orders were imposed. While obviously there are similarities to the sample examined in the first section of the report, because of the different bases of the samples no comparisons are drawn between them.

---

20   As this section of the report deals with people who moved from the criminal justice system to the healthcare system following sentence (albeit while continuing to be monitored by the Home Office), and who spent the period preceding discharge in hospital, they are referred to predominantly as patients, rather than as offenders.

21   The sample consists only of people on section 37/41 orders and NOT restricted patients on transfers under section 47 of the MHA 1983, or those detained under the Criminal Procedures (Insanity) Act 1964. Due to their files being unavailable, 5 cases were not included.

Details of the restriction orders

Three-fifths of the sample were sentenced under the 1959, rather than the 1983, Mental Health Act (MHA)[22]. The restriction orders were made between 1961 and 1989, (the modal years being 1986 and 1987, although nearly three-quarters of the orders had been imposed by the end of 1985).

Of the total sample of 391 cases, all but seven of the restriction orders were made without limit of time. Those that were time-limited were made for periods ranging from one to five years, the mode being three years.

Type of mental disorder

Full information on primary diagnosis at time of sentence was not always available. Because of the incompleteness of the data, the MHA categories were used to classify the types of disorder.

Table 5.1 below shows the MHA categories.

Table 5.1   MHA category (when discharged from hospital)[23]

MHA category	%	N
Mental Illness	64	250
Psychopathic Disorder	24	92
Mental Impairment*	10	39
Mental Illness + Psychopathic Disorder	2	7
Mental Illness + Mental Impairment	1	2
Psychopathic Disorder + Mental Impairment	<1	1

*   Notes: Because of rounding, the percentages do not sum to 100. The 'mental impairment' category includes two people categorised under 'severe mental impairment'.

Because the mixed diagnosis groups were very small, they were merged with the principal disorder groups to create three main categories for the purposes of analysis. Thus, the mental illness + psychopathic disorder group was included in the psychopathic disorder category, while the mental illness + mental impairment and the psychopathic disorder + mental impairment groups were included in the mental impairment category.

22   Under the 1959 MHA, the criteria for a restriction order (while still aiming to protect the public) did not include a reference to 'serious harm' – that was added by the 1983 MHA.
23   At some stage during their hospitalisation, five patients initially classified as mentally ill were reclassified to psychopathic disorder, one in the psychopathic disorder category was reclassified to mental illness, and one patient classified as being mentally impaired was reclassified to mental illness.

Demographic information

Age

The range of ages when the restriction orders were imposed was 14 to 69 years, the average age being 31 years. Two-fifths of the sample were aged 30 or under, and a further two-fifths were aged between 31 and 50 years.

Sex

Over four-fifths of the sample were male and just 17 per cent (n=66) female.

Ethnicity

Of the 365 patients for whom ethnicity data were available, 81 per cent were white, 15 per cent were black, three per cent were Asian, and one per cent were from other ethnic groups.

Type of hospital

Following sentence, nearly 60 per cent of the sample were sent to a special hospital, a quarter went first to medium secure units, and 16 per cent went to local hospitals or interim secure units. This information was unavailable or unclear in two per cent of cases.

Previous psychiatric treatment

Over two-thirds of the sample (67%) had been psychiatric in-patients at least once before the restriction order was imposed; nine per cent had been previously treated just as an out-patient, and three per cent had seen their GP for psychiatric reasons. Only a fifth of the sample had experienced no known previous psychiatric treatment.

Of those who had previously been in-patients, just under a half (49%, n=129) had been admitted under a Section of the MHA 1959 or 1983 at some stage.

Index Offence

As Table 5.2 shows, just under half the sample had been convicted of manslaughter, attempted murder or GBH. Overall, nearly two-thirds had been convicted of a violent offence. Convictions for arson or sexual offences were also common. Mentally ill patients were significantly the most likely to have been convicted of a violent index offence (especially very serious violence), followed by the psychopathically disordered and then the mentally impaired, while the converse was true for a sexual index offence.

Table 5.2 Main index offence

Main offence	%	N
Manslaughter	22	84
Attempted murder	4	16
GBH	23	89
Other assaults and threats to kill	10	42
Arson	17	68
Rape/Buggery	5	20
Other sexual offences	9	36
Robbery	3	10
Other serious offences*	4	14
Other offences*	3	12

* Notes: 'Other serious offences' comprises aggravated burglary, burglary, abduction, false imprisonment, and firearms offences. 'Other offences' includes theft, criminal damage, possession of an offensive weapon, and other public order offences.

Just under a third of the sample had been convicted of more than one offence.

Given the serious nature of most of the index offences, it is not surprising that the degree of injury caused to victims was often severe: nearly half of the sample had either killed someone or caused serious injury (as defined on page 13). In just under a further quarter of cases some injury had been caused, and in about another tenth there was potential for serious injury although no-one was actually harmed. In only 14 per cent of cases did the offender not cause or threaten any injury.

Relationship to victim

Of the 320 cases (72%) where a direct victim of the index offence could be identified, in nearly a third the victim was either the offender's partner (former or current) or a family member. A friend or acquaintance of the offender was the victim in a further 27 per cent of cases. A third of victims were strangers, and six per cent were officials (doctors, nurses, police officers, etc.). In five cases the offender's relationship with the victim was not clear.

Sexual motive

A sexual motive to the index offence was apparent in a fifth of cases. In three-quarters of these cases, the index offence had been a sexual one.

Previous convictions

Seventy per cent of the sample had previous convictions when sentenced. Of these, nearly two-thirds (43% of the total sample) had at least one previous conviction for either a violent or a sexual offence.

There was a strong association between a previous conviction for a sexual offence, and a sexual index offence, and some association (although not quite statistically significant) between previous convictions for violence and a violent index offence.

Of the different disorder groups, the psychopathically disordered were significantly the most likely to have previous convictions for any type of offence and reportedly to have engaged in dangerous behaviour that did not result in conviction.

Key points

- Of a sample of 391 restricted patients who were followed up after their discharge from hospital, nearly three-quarters had been categorised as being mentally ill when sentenced to a restricted hospital order under either the 1959 or the 1983 MHA.

- Nearly half of the sample had been convicted of either manslaughter or causing GBH, with convictions for other violent offences and arson also being common. The majority of offenders had previous convictions, often including ones for violent or sexual offences.

- In addition to widespread criminal histories, previous contact with psychiatric services was also very prevalent, with over two-thirds of the sample having been in-patients before.

6 Discharge from hospital

The structure of a restriction order, with its conditional discharge system, emphasises that the assessment and management of risk is a continuous and long-term exercise. Nevertheless, the decision to discharge from hospital remains a crucial one. Although, of course, public safety will be a primary consideration in most discharge decisions, removing a patient from a structured (and often secure) therapeutic environment and allowing him or her to live with more freedom in the community on a permanent basis presents the first real test of the work done to control or negate the risk presented by the patient.

The data relating to the discharge decision were drawn solely from information in MHU files. More qualitative and detailed information on the way in which MHRTs approach discharge decisions is provided by Peay (1989) and Hepworth (1985).

Mode of discharge

Restricted patients can be discharged from hospital either by a MHRT or with the consent of the Home Secretary.

Nearly two-thirds (62%, n=241) of the sample were discharged by a MHRT, with the remaining 150 patients being discharged with the consent of the Home Secretary.

Form of discharge

Of the sample, 370 were first discharged conditionally, and 21 absolutely. Discharge was deferred in 28 per cent of cases, the purpose of deferment being to allow conditions for discharge (such as accommodation upon release) to be prepared. The average length of time between the initial decision to grant (deferred) discharge and actual discharge was just over 10 months, with periods ranging from under one month to nearly six years (this latter case involved a mentally impaired patient with very special needs). Half of the deferred cases were actually discharged within six months and nearly three-quarters within one year, although 12 per cent spent at least two years awaiting discharge from hospital. The length of the deferment period was significantly longer for mentally impaired patients than for mentally ill or psychopathically disordered patients.

Seventeen of the 21 absolute discharges were directed by MHRTs. In fourteen of those cases the MHRT ruled that the patient in question no longer suffered from a mental disorder within the meaning of the MHA, while in the other three cases it held that it was not appropriate for the patient to remain liable to recall.

The Home Office absolutely discharged four patients. Two of them had been reconvicted for offences committed while in hospital, one being given another restricted hospital order and one an eight-year custodial sentence. The latter, along with another patient who was remanded in custody for further alleged offences, was said to have an untreatable personality disorder, and the RMO urged absolute discharge. The fourth patient had absconded from hospital and been absent for three years.

Overall, ten of those absolutely discharged were classified as mentally ill, five as psychopathically disordered, and six as mentally impaired.

Unescorted leave and place of residence at time of discharge

Ninety-three per cent of patients had some unescorted leave of absence from the hospital (granted under Section 17 MHA 1983) before discharge. In the great majority of these cases (90%), leave passed successfully without any serious problems or mishaps. However, in a tenth of cases unescorted leave was thought to have been either only partially successful (30 cases), or even unsuccessful (6 cases). This was not solely due to failures on the patient's part (e.g. the patient drinking excessively, or absconding), but sometimes because of difficulties with relatives or living arrangements while on leave.

In fact, nearly a third (n=116) of all patients were living away from the hospital site (either at private addresses, hostels or rehabilitative units) when their discharge was granted. Of those residing in hospital at the time of the discharge decision, half were in local hospitals, 36 per cent were in RSUs/MSUs, and 14 per cent were in special hospitals. Four offenders were in prison when discharged and one offender had absconded from hospital. PD patients were significantly more likely to have been in a special hospital at time of discharge than mentally ill or mentally impaired patients (20% versus 6% and 7% respectively).

Length of detention and age at discharge

Table 6.1 shows the distribution of time spent in hospital before discharge as a proportion of each disorder group and of the whole sample.

Table 6.1: Length of detention in hospital by type of disorder

Time in hospital	Mental Illness	Psychopathic Disorder	Mental Impairment	TOTAL
0-2 years	34%	7%	5%	**24%**
3-5 years	21%	22%	5%	**20%**
6-8 years	15%	17%	14%	**15%**
9-11 years	11%	11%	7%	**11%**
12-14 years	7%	14%	14%	**9%**
15 years or over	12%	29%	55%	**21%**
AVERAGE	**6 years**	**10 years**	**14 years**	**8 years**

The full range of time spent in hospital before discharge was from under one year to 26 years. Eleven patients (all in the mental illness group) spent under one year in hospital.

As Table 6.1 indicates, mentally impaired patients were detained significantly longer on average than either psychopathically disordered patients or mentally ill patients. Of the different disorder groups, those suffering from mental illnesses will typically be the most likely to improve (and in many cases, improve most quickly) in response to treatment, which probably accounts for the shorter time that they as a group spent in hospital. However, it is possible that those patients in the PD and mental impairment groups may have been detained for longer because proportionately more of them had committed sexual offences: patients whose index offence was a sexual one spent a significantly longer average period in hospital (nearly 13 years) than patients whose index offence was of a different nature (8 years).

The average age at discharge was just over 40 years, with a range of 18 to 76 years. Psychopathically disordered patients were on average significantly younger at discharge (37 years) than the mentally ill (41 years) and the mentally impaired (42 years).

Home Office discharges

Of the 150 offenders first discharged from hospital with the consent of the Home Office, 97 per cent were discharged conditionally and the remaining three per cent absolutely.

Given that Home Office discharges will almost always be precipitated by a request from the Responsible Medical Officer (RMO), it was not surprising that there was clear evidence of the RMO supporting discharge in all but four of these cases. The reasons given for Home Office discharges were invariably the receipt of favourable reports from supervisors and, in particular, the patient successfully undertaking a period of leave of absence from hospital. Overall, 55 per cent of those discharged by the Home Office were living away from hospital when the discharge decision was made. All but seven of the patients discharged with the consent of the Home Office had been on unescorted leave before discharge (three of the latter had reoffended while still in hospital), and in only one case had that leave been unsuccessful (also a patient who reoffended while still in hospital).

Nearly three-quarters of those discharged by the Home Office came under the MHA category of mental illness. Twenty-one per cent were psychopathically disordered, and seven per cent were mentally impaired.

There was evidence that 13 per cent of patients had engaged in behaviour that was harmful (or potentially harmful) to others during their period in hospital for which they were not prosecuted or convicted.

MHRT discharges

Of the 241 patients first discharged from hospital by MHRTs, 93 per cent (n=224) of the discharges were conditional, with the remaining seven per cent being absolute.

Fifty-nine per cent of these offenders were in the MHA category of mental illness. A further 28 per cent were psychopathically disordered, and 13 per cent were mentally impaired.

In 47 per cent of cases, the sole reason given by MHRTs for discharge was that the patient's disorder was not of a nature or a degree warranting detention[24]. Detention no longer being necessary for the health or safety of the patient or for the protection of others[25] was the sole reason given for discharge in four per cent of cases. In seven per cent of cases (five out of these 16 were conditional discharges), discharge was made on the basis of there being no evidence of any mental disorder within the meaning of the MHA 1983. In the remaining 42 per cent of cases, a mixture of reasons for discharge was given – usually a combination of the first two.

Although detention being unnecessary for the protection of others was not a common reason for discharge by itself, it featured in 43 per cent of all MHRT

---

24   Section 72(1)(b)(i), MHA 1983.
25   Section 72(1)(b)(ii), MHA 1983.

discharges. Overall, 58 per cent of the written records of MHRT decisions explicitly indicated some discussion of risk at the hearing.

As the Home Office was not itself proposing to discharge these patients at that time, by definition it opposed discharge. Nonetheless, it was clear from the files that there were *degrees* of Home Office opposition. In six per cent of tribunal discharges, the Home Office sent a statement to the MHRT strongly opposing discharge; notably, discharge was supported by the RMO in each of these cases. Opposition to discharge was clearly expressed in a further 80 per cent of cases, although in over one-third of these cases that opposition was conveyed in a more qualified fashion, usually taking the form of a statement that discharge was opposed until the patient had shown some sign of further improvement. However, in 14 per cent of cases the Home Office did not expressly oppose discharge in its statements to the tribunal (usually the statement was neutral as to discharge). In two-fifths of those cases the patient had already been granted a period of leave of absence from hospital by the Home Office.

The RMO supported discharge in nearly nine-tenths of MHRT discharges, including 10 per cent (n=20) of cases where the RMO proposed absolute discharge. Of the latter, only seven did actually result in an absolute discharge. However, there were still three per cent of MHRT cases where the RMO was neutral about discharge and nine per cent of cases where the RMO did not support discharge in his or her report to the tribunal. In most of the latter cases the RMO's opposition was conditional rather than absolute, i.e. the RMO thought that the patient should receive further treatment before being considered ready for discharge. Of course, it is possible that the RMO gave a different opinion when actually appearing at the MHRT than that expressed in his or her report.

Twenty-six per cent of the patients discharged by MHRTs were described in reports as having engaged in behaviour which was harmful (or potentially harmful) to others at some stage in their period in hospital for which they were not prosecuted or convicted.

Differences between Home Office and MHRT discharges

The main differences between patients discharged by either MHRTs or with the consent of the Home Secretary are summarised in Table 6.2.

Table 6.2 Main differences between Home Office and MHRT discharges

	Home Office discharges	MHRT discharges
MHA category	72% mental illness 21% PD 7% mental impairment	59% mental illness 28% PD 13% mental impairment
Absolutely discharged*	3%	7%
Actually resident in hospital at time of discharge	45%	86%
Any incident of harmful behaviour while in hospital	13%	26%

*   Note: the difference in the proportions absolutely discharged was not quite statistically significant (p=.06)

There were no significant differences between Home Office and MHRT discharges in respect of type of index offence, extent of previous convictions, or the length of time patients spent in hospital.

Key points

• The great majority of the sample were discharged conditionally rather than absolutely from hospital. Nearly two-thirds of patients were discharged by MHRTs.

• Nearly half of patients spent five years or less in hospital before discharge, although more than a fifth were detained for 15 years or more.

• The RMO supported discharge in nearly nine-tenths of MHRTs cases, whereas the Home Office routinely opposed discharge in MHRT cases.

• Proportionately more of Home Office-discharged patients were mentally ill, while more of the patients discharged by MHRTs were psychopathically disordered. Greater proportions of MHRT-discharged patients were absolutely discharged, were actually resident in hospital at time of discharge, and had engaged in behaviour harmful to others while in hospital.

7 Circumstances following discharge

This chapter describes the social circumstances of the 370 conditionally discharged patients[26] following their discharge from hospital. The data were drawn from information contained in patients' MHU files. Social circumstances are an important consideration, not only because they are an indication of a patient's progress following discharge from hospital, but also because of the effect that situational factors can have upon the degree of risk a patient poses to others (see, for example, Monahan and Steadman, 1994).

Virtually all patients had a condition of residence and/or conditions of receiving social and psychiatric supervision imposed upon their discharge. A smaller number (14%) had other conditions imposed, such as a condition not to go to certain places or not to associate with children, for example.

Living arrangements

Just over half (54%) the conditionally discharged patients were initially discharged to live in a hostel or group home. Discharge to the patient's own home was also quite common (20% of cases), as was discharge to the parental or other relatives' home (16%). Most of the remaining 10 per cent of patients were first discharged to sheltered housing or lodgings with a landlord.

The living arrangements of nearly three-quarters of patients altered during the study period. In some cases this resulted from a patient's offending or disruptive behaviour, or from the arrangements being somehow unsuitable for the patient. But the most common reasons for change were positive ones, such as the patient being able to move to more independent accommodation.

Marital status and relationships with others

Eighteen patients were already married at the time of their discharge from hospital. Just over a third of patients (34%, n=127) became involved in a

---

26   Details were unavailable for the 21 absolutely discharged patients.

steady relationship during their conditional discharge, including 33 patients who got married and another 36 who cohabited with their partner. PD patients were signifiantly the most likely to have formed such relationships: 47 per cent of them did so, compared to 39 per cent of patients in the mental impairment category, and 29 per cent of those in the mental illness group. There were no notable differences by sex or ethnicity.

In addition to relationships with partners, over half the sample had regular contact with members of their family, and nearly a further third had at least some contact. Social contact with friends, other acquaintances and workmates was also enjoyed by most of the sample. Nevertheless, nearly a quarter of the sample were described by their supervisors at some stage as having problems in socialising.

Employment

Four-fifths of those conditionally discharged were engaged in an occupation at some stage during the study period, such as paid employment, voluntary work, studying or training schemes. Over a quarter had full-time employment. Patients in the psychopathic disorder category were significantly more likely to have secured paid employment than mentally ill or mentally impaired patients: 61 per cent versus 35 per cent and 39 per cent, respectively. Again, there were no notable differences by sex or ethnicity.

Psychiatric treatment and non-recall hospital admissions

Sixty per cent of conditionally discharged patients either remained mentally stable during the study period or suffered just minor incidents of deterioration.

The mental state of the remaining 40 per cent patients, however, deteriorated sufficiently at some stage to require additional intervention. Most commonly this took the form of either a non-recall hospital admission[27], medication being prescribed or increased, or recall to hospital (the latter is discussed in Chapter 10). Almost half of the mentally ill patients received some such intervention, compared to about a third of the psychopathically disordered and the mentally impaired – a statistically significant difference. Patients from black, Asian and other ethnic groups were more likely to have required psychiatric intervention than white patients, although the difference was not statistically significant.

---

27 'Non-recall hospital admission' refers to all psychiatric in-patient admissions not resulting from formal recall to hospital under section 42(3) MHA 1983.

Seventy per cent of conditionally discharged patients were prescribed medication during the study period, the great majority of whom were taking medication throughout this time. Those patients in the mental illness category were significantly more likely than the other two MHA groups to have been on medication: 88 per cent of the mentally ill compared to 35 per cent of the PD and 39 per cent of the mentally impaired.

Just over a third of those conditionally discharged had at least one non-recall admission to hospital. These admissions were often only for a few days (although some lasted weeks) and usually on a voluntary basis, although a quarter of those admitted were compulsorily treated under a civil Section of the MHA 1983 at some stage (usually Sections 2 or 3). Although the primary reason for admission was concern about the patient's mental state, admission was sometimes prompted by other events or crises, such as the patient unexpectedly becoming homeless, or appearing to become a risk to others.

Problems with supervision

While certainly not an easy time for any patient, the period of supervision progressed fairly well for most of them. However, 43 patients (12% of those conditionally discharged) appeared to cause significant problems for their supervisors (other than by refusing medication), ranging from persistently failing to co-operate with conditions of discharge to absconding from the country. A further 63 patients caused some problems for their supervisors, albeit of a lesser nature or frequency, making a total of nearly a third of all conditionally discharged patients who caused difficulties with their supervision. Male patients were about twice as likely as female patients, and patients from black, Asian or other ethnic groups were nearly three times as likely as white patients, to have been described as causing problems with supervision. There were no significant differences in this respect between the three main MHA categories.

Problems caused by drug and alcohol misuse were reportedly experienced at some stage by 88 patients (24% of those conditionally discharged): 58 were described as having misused alcohol, 18 had misused drugs, and 12 both drugs and alcohol. Those patients in the mental illness category were significantly more likely to be described as having misused drugs than those in the psychopathic disorder or mental impairment categories, although the numbers in each category were small. There was no difference between the three main MHA categories when it came to problems with alcohol.

Victimisation and self-harm

Fifty-nine patients (16%) reported being victimised during the study period. They most frequently alleged that they were victims of violent or sexual assaults (33 cases) or threatening behaviour (14 cases), although reports of theft, burglary, and criminal damage were not uncommon.

Interestingly, those who were reportedly the victims of a violent offence or threatening behaviour were significantly more likely than those who did not report such victimisations either to have been reconvicted of a serious offence or to have been involved in a harmful incident (see Chapters 8 and 9): 37 per cent versus 13 per cent. One possible explanation for this is that there was sometimes mention in MHU files of disputes between patients and their acquaintances (particularly in hostels), occasionally resulting in aggressive behaviour by both parties.

In addition, those patients described as causing problems with their supervision were significantly more likely to have been the victim of a violent offence, as were those patients considered to have a problem socialising with others.

There was very little difference in levels of victimisation between the three main MHA groups. Women were more likely than men to report that they had been victims of an offence, while black patients were more likely to have reported being a victim both of any type of offence and an offence against the person than white or Asian patients. Neither of the differences were statistically significant, however.

In addition to victimisation by others, four patients killed themselves during the follow-up period and another 43 deliberately harmed themselves in some way (23 of those cases involved serious harm, such as overdoses). Twenty-one per cent of female patients harmed themselves, compared to 11 per cent of the male patients, a statistically significant difference.

The end of the follow-up

By the end of December 1994, 45 per cent of the conditionally discharged patients were no longer under restrictions. Fifty-eight per cent of these had been absolutely discharged by MHRT, while a further 30 per cent had been absolutely discharged by the Home Office. Of the remainder, 14 offenders had died, and in six cases the time limit on their restrictions had expired.

Mentally ill patients were the most likely still to be under restrictions by the end of the study (59% were); psychopathically disordered patients the least likely (43% were). There were no significant differences in terms of sex or ethnicity as to whether patients had been absolutely discharged from their restriction orders by the end of the follow-up, although significantly more of those who had been described as causing problems with supervision, or had reportedly caused or threatened harm to others, were still restricted than those who had not caused such difficulties (even if not still in hospital on recall).

For those who had been absolutely discharged from their order (discounting those who were absolutely discharged straight from hospital), an average of just over 14 years had passed since their order had been imposed.

Overall, patients with mental impairment spent, on average, a significantly longer period under restrictions than patients from the other disorder categories: just over 21 years, compared to just over 12 years for mentally ill patients, and nearly 16 years for psychopathically disordered patients.

Key points

- Despite the obvious difficulties of resettling into the community after what was often a lengthy period in hospital, most conditionally discharged patients reintegrated well, gradually living more independently, obtaining employment or training of some sort, and maintaining regular social contact with others.

- However, a sizeable minority of patients (especially the mentally ill) suffered deterioration in their mental state at some stage (often leading to hospital admission), or created difficulties with supervision. Furthermore, nearly a quarter of patients misused drugs or alcohol at some stage during their conditional discharge.

- Nearly half the conditionally discharged patients had been absolutely discharged by the end of the study period, having spent on average just over 14 years under their restriction order. Those in the mental illness category were the most likely of the three main disorder groups still to be under restrictions, while mentally impaired patients had spent the longest period under restrictions.

- About a sixth of patients reported offences against them, often of a violent or sexual nature. As well as victimisation by others, 43 patients deliberately harmed themselves, while four committed suicide.

8 Reconvictions

As restriction orders are imposed because of the risk an offender is believed to pose to others, reconvictions will obviously be a principal outcome of interest for restricted patients following their discharge from hospital. Numerous reconviction studies, often of particular populations of mentally disordered offenders, have generally found that such offenders have relatively low reconviction rates[28]. A recent comparison (Home Office, 1997b) indicated that, on the whole, discharged restricted patients have lower reconviction rates than non-disordered offenders released from prison (except for life licensees).

The emphasis of the restriction order on the prevention of *serious* harm means that the reconvictions of primary interest should be those for offences which caused, or threatened, serious harm to others.

Because the patients were discharged over four different years, but were all followed until the end of 1994 for reconviction purposes, the length of follow-up time varied between patients. The average period of follow-up was 5.9 years, counting from date of discharge from hospital up until the end of the study period. Information on reconvictions was drawn from both the patients' MHU files and Offenders Index data.

How many patients were reconvicted?

Table 8.1 shows the number of patients who were reconvicted during the study period and the stage at which they were first reconvicted, expressed as percentages of the total sample.

---

28   See Murray (1989) for an overview.

Table 8.1 Reconvictions during study period

	First reconvicted during conditional discharge		First reconvicted after absolute discharge		TOTAL	
	N	*%*	*N*	*%*	*N*	*%*
Reconvicted of any offence	34	9	14	3	48	12
Reconvicted of a serious offence	16	4	5	1	21	5

A further seven patients were reconvicted for offences committed *before* discharge from hospital. In the following analysis, they were not counted as having been reconvicted.

Table 8.1 shows that only a small minority (12%, n=48) of the sample were convicted of an offence committed after discharge from hospital by the end of 1994. Twenty-one of these reconvictions (equating to 5% of the sample) were categorised as 'serious' because of the harm that they either caused or threatened to others. The offences comprising these serious convictions were taken to be all violent and sexual offences (excluding common assault, assaulting a police officer and indecent exposure), threats to kill, arson, aggravated burglary and abduction. This definition is similar to that employed by Bailey and MacCulloch (1992), and was felt to be more appropriate for this group of offenders than the narrower category of 'grave offences'[29] used in Home Office Statistical Bulletins.

Offences for which reconvicted

Table 8.2 below shows the most serious offences for which discharged patients were reconvicted. A third of the 48 reoffenders were reconvicted on more than one occasion during the follow-up period.

---

29 Defined in Home Office Statistical Bulletins as covering all indictable-only offences which have a maximum sentence of life imprisonment. These are mainly offences of: homicide; serious wounding; rape; buggery; aggravated burglary; robbery; and arson.

Table 8.2 Most serious reconvictions

Main offence	Number
Serious Offences (n=21)	
Manslaughter	1
Attempted murder	2
GBH or ABH	4
Rape	3
Indecent assault or Gross Indecency	3
Arson	1
Threats to kill	3
Robbery	2
Abduction	1
Aggravated burglary	1
Other Offences (n=27)	
Burglary	5
Theft	10
Criminal damage	2
Public Order	2
Other offences*	8
TOTAL	48

* Note: 'Other offences' comprise indecent exposure, possession of drugs, making hoax calls, cruelty to an animal, and driving without insurance.

Although the numbers involved were too small to allow useful statistical analysis, a comparison of the nature of the serious reconviction offences with the offenders' respective index offences showed that they were broadly similar. Thus, of the 13 serious reconvictions for offences of a violent nature (violent assaults, robbery, threats to kill and aggravated burglary), in nine cases the offender's index offence had also been violent. Similarly, five of the seven offenders with a sexual reconviction (this includes the sexually motivated abduction) had a sexual index offence, and the offender reconvicted of arson had been initially convicted of the same offence.

Victims and injuries caused

Further details on the offence leading to reconviction were available for 17 of the 21 serious reoffenders. Almost half (n=8) of these 17 serious reoffenders had committed their offence against a stranger. The remainder had offended against either a partner or family member, or acquaintance. None of the victims were officials.

Death or serious injury was caused to the victim in four of the serious reconviction cases, and some injury caused in another five cases. One offence (aggravated burglary) nearly led to serious injury as the result of an attempted knife attack, and another offence (arson) led to serious property damage, but no injury. The offences in the remaining cases (sexual offences, threats to kill and robbery) did not result in physical injury to the victim.

Court disposal

Of the 21 serious reoffenders, only four received further Section 37/41 orders when sentenced, while 16 were given custodial sentences for periods ranging between three months and life (four received life sentences) and one offender received a community penalty. Most of the 27 less serious reoffenders were either fined, given probation orders, or discharged by the court.

Type of discharge

As with a number of previous follow-up studies of discharged restricted patients (see Bailey and MacCulloch, 1992), proportionately more of those first released from hospital by absolute discharge were reconvicted of any offence (19%, n=4) than those conditionally discharged (12%, n=44), although the numbers involved are small and the difference was not statistically significant. There was no difference between the two types of discharge for serious reconvictions, with five per cent of both conditionally and absolutely discharged patients being reconvicted of serious offences.

MHA categories

Of the three main MHA categories, those patients in the PD category were both the most likely to have been reconvicted of a serious offence – nine per cent compared to five per cent of the mentally ill and none of the mentally impaired – and the most likely to have been reconvicted of any offence – 17 per cent compared to 10 per cent of the mentally ill group and 12 per cent of the mentally impaired. These differences were not statistically significant, probably because of the small numbers involved.

Mode of discharge

Although proportionately more of those first discharged from hospital by MHRTs (15%) were reconvicted during the study than those discharged by the Home Office (9%), this difference was not statistically significant. More importantly, for reconviction for serious offences, the proportions were very similar: six per cent of MHRT discharges, compared to five per cent of those discharged with the consent of the Home Secretary.

For those patients discharged by a MHRT, there was no association between serious reconviction and whether or not the record of the tribunal hearing indicated a discussion of risk, nor whether or not the RMO had supported discharge.

Sex

While men were more likely to be reconvicted than women, the difference in reconviction rates between the sexes (6% of men reconvicted of a serious offence compared to 2% of women, and 13% of men reconvicted of any offence compared to 8% of women) was not statistically significant.

Ethnicity

There were no significant variations in reconviction rates between the different ethnic groups.

Age

The average age at discharge from hospital of all 48 patients reconvicted was significantly lower than those patients not reconvicted – 34 years versus nearly 41 years – while the average age at discharge of those who were reconvicted of serious offences was lower than the average age of those who were not – 35 years versus 40 years – although not quite significantly so.

Time periods

The average length of time between discharge from hospital and committing the most serious offence[30] for which reconvicted (for all patients reconvicted) was 2.5 years, although Figure 8.1 below shows that the cumulative proportion of the sample who were reconvicted over time rose steadily to the four year mark (the maximum amount of time that the entire sample spent in the community).

---

30 Using data from MHU files, we were usually able to obtain a date for the actual offence; in the few cases where this was not available, the date of conviction was used instead. This information was missing in one case.

Figure 8.1 Cumulative percentage of sample reconvicted

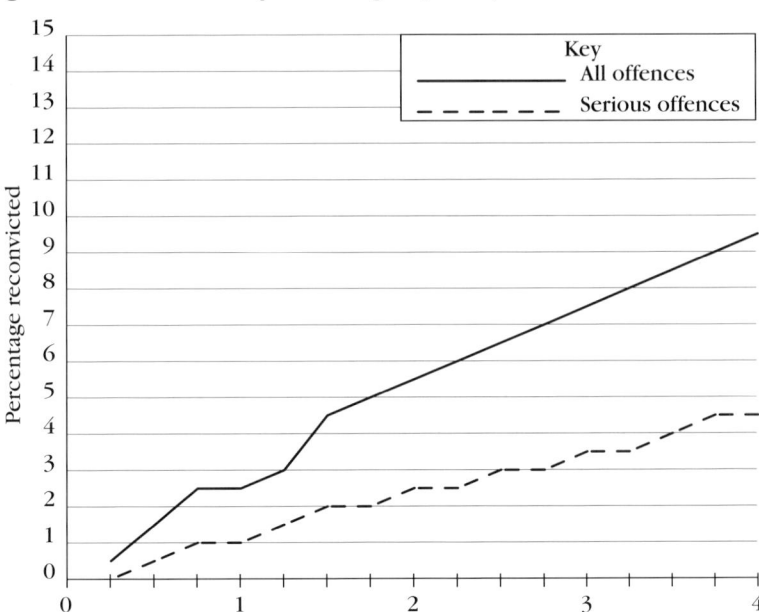

A further nine patients reoffended (three seriously) after more than four years in the community, although none reoffended after more than six years. Nevertheless, this indicates the importance of employing follow-up periods of at least four years and preferably more for reconviction studies of this kind.

Mentally ill patients (but not PD patients) who were reconvicted of a serious offence spent a significantly shorter average time detained in hospital before discharge (four years) than did those who were not reconvicted (seven years).

Index offence and previous convictions

While there was no significant association between type of index offence and being reconvicted for a serious offence, 11 per cent of those who had a sexual motive to their index offence (which in most cases was a sexual offence) were reconvicted of a serious offence, compared to just five per cent of those who did not have such a motive.

Those with previous convictions for violent or sexual offences were three times as likely to be reconvicted of a serious offence (9%, n=15) as those who did not have such previous convictions (3%, n=6).

Similarly, those with previous convictions for *any* type of offence were significantly more likely to be reconvicted of *any* type of offence: 16 per cent of those with previous convictions were reconvicted, compared to just 4 per cent of those with no previous convictions prior to their index offence.

Other factors associated with reconviction

For the 370 conditionally discharged patients, more information was available from their MHU files about a range of other factors that were associated with reconviction.

Those patients who were described by their supervisors as causing problems with supervision were significantly more likely to be reconvicted of a serious offence than those not so described: 13 per cent compared to two per cent. Problems with alcohol or drug misuse also had a significant association with reconviction: 13 per cent of those described as having these problems were reconvicted of a serious offence, compared to just three per cent of other patients.

Forty-eight conditionally discharged patients were reportedly involved in incidents that caused or threatened harm to others, but that did not result in conviction (see Chapter 5). These incidents were also significantly associated with serious reconvictions: 15 per cent of those reconvicted of serious offences were involved in such incidents, compared to just four per cent of those patients who were not. In addition, the 115 patients about whom supervisors expressed fears or concerns about possible dangerousness (as distinct from any incidents which actually caused or seriously threatened harm to others) were twice as likely to have been reconvicted of a serious offence as those who did not cause such concerns, although the latter difference was not statistically significant.

Of the 16 patients reconvicted of serious offences during their conditional discharge, 10 had experienced some form of social upheaval in the six months prior to their offence (ranging from disrupted living arrangements to problems in relationships with others), and which in four cases had seemed to contribute to the subsequent offending.

Finally, those 148 patients whose mental state deteriorated during conditional discharge to the point where some psychiatric intervention had to be made, were three times more likely than those who did not deteriorate to have been reconvicted of a serious offence: nine per cent compared to three per cent.

Predicting reoffending

In addition to the above bivariate analysis of factors associated with reconviction, a model combining several factors to predict the probability of reconviction of a serious offence after discharge from hospital was attempted.

It was not possible to build a model that could satisfactorily predict more than 15 per cent of the reconvictions, reflecting not only the difficulties of trying to predict a rare outcome (i.e. being reconvicted of a serious offence), but also that whether a patient was reconvicted depended not just upon whether he or she reoffended, but also upon the reaction to the offending behaviour on the part of supervisors, the Home Office, witnesses or victims, police, CPS, and the courts, and other intervening factors that could not be catered for in the model.

However, a model to predict serious reconvictions or being involved in harmful behaviour towards others which did not lead to conviction (see chapter 5) was more successful. Appendix D shows the results of this analysis.

The model was able to predict 52 per cent of those patients who did behave in a harmful way towards others (whether or not convicted for that behaviour). The variables in the most efficient model were:

- having a previous conviction for a sexual offence and a sexually-motivated index offence

- causing problems with supervision (as defined above)

- mental state deteriorating to the point where psychiatric intervention was required

- misusing drugs or alcohol.

It should be noted that the presence of the latter three variables does not necessarily mean that the incident of reoffending was actually connected to deteriorating mental state, drug or alcohol misuse, or failing to co-operate with supervision, but that these were factors which occurred at some stage, and so can perhaps be seen as general indicators of patients' problems with supervision and their instability.

These results are not surprising, although it was interesting that a history of sexual offending was a significant predictor of subsequent harmful behaviour (whether or not resulting in conviction), but previous violent offences were not. Previous sexual offending seemed to be associated with psychopathic disorder: significantly more PD patients with a history of sexual offending behaved harmfully after discharge than their mentally ill or learning disabled counterparts.

The difficulties and dangers of trying to predict harmful behaviour are widely reported (see Walker, 1996, for example) and were illustrated in this study by the model's seven per cent rate of 'false positives'[31] and its ability to predict only just over half the total of serious reconvictions and harmful incidents. Furthermore, some of the recent inquiries into homicides committed by mentally disordered people have concluded that, even with hindsight, it was not possible to predict the violence that occurred (see the Jason Mitchell Inquiry (Blom-Cooper, 1996) for example).

Discussion

While any further offending by restricted patients is a matter of great concern, a reconviction rate of five per cent for serious offences among a sample who have been followed up for between four to seven years is a modest one.

The figures in this study (drawn from data about reconvictions contained in patients' files) are confirmed by those given in a recent Home Office Statistical Bulletin (Home Office, 1997b) which are drawn from the Offenders Index. These indicated an 11 per cent overall reconviction rate (for any type of offence) by the end of 1995 for those restricted patients first discharged from hospital between 1987 and 1990, including a three per cent reconviction rate for grave offences (as defined in footnote 29, page 68). Employing a similar definition (although not an identical one, as offences were categorised in a slightly different way in this study than on the Offenders Index) revealed that our sample had a reconviction rate of three per cent for these grave offences.

The slight discrepancy in the overall reconviction rate for the two samples is probably due to the Offenders Index not recording some summary offences and the samples being slightly different (the Offenders Index sample includes restricted patients detained under Section 47 MHA 1983 and the provisions of the Criminal Procedures (Insanity) Act 1964, for example). What is notable is that the reconviction rates for both these samples appear to be lower than those for restricted patients first discharged from hospital between 1972 and 1986, of whom 31 per cent were reconvicted of a standard list offence within five years of discharge, including six per cent reconvicted of a grave offence (Home Office, 1997). To some extent, this

---

31   In this instance, 'false positives' refers to those patients who were predicted to reoffend but who did not actually do so.

decline in reconvictions over time probably reflects changes in prosecution policy towards mentally disordered offenders[32], although it may also indicate more effective post-discharge supervision, or changes in behaviour by discharged restricted patients.

The low reconviction rate among this sample meant that it was difficult to distinguish significantly by broad *categories* of offender (i.e. whether discharged by a MHRT or by the Home Office, or MHA disorder classification) those who were reconvicted of serious offences from those who were not. This emphasises the need also to focus attention upon the psychological traits and external situational factors that may dispose individual discharged patients to reoffend. Indeed, much recent research into violence committed by mentally disordered people is increasingly looking at the effects of factors like impulsiveness, reactions to provocation, empathy with others, and the nature of delusions and hallucinations (see Steadman et al., in Hodgins, 1993). Thus, while key variables such as a history of violence, or drug or alcohol problems, remain very important considerations in determining broadly what degree of risk to others a patient is likely to pose, the most precise indicators as to future risk are likely to lie in the particular details and circumstances of a patient's case. The issue of predicting offending, and its implications for the discharge of patients from hospital, is discussed again in the concluding chapter.

Key points

- Five per cent of the sample were reconvicted of a serious offence (one which either caused or threatened harm to others) during the follow-up. Twelve per cent of the sample were reconvicted of any type of offence.

- There were significant associations between serious reconvictions and previous convictions for sexual or violent offences, problems with drug or alcohol misuse, and supervisory difficulties, but not for sex, ethnicity, MHA category or mode of discharge.

- Attempts to predict the likelihood of a patient harming others (whether or not subsequently convicted of this behaviour) indicated that patients who had a history of sexual offending, caused problems with supervision, had problems with alcohol or drug misuse, and suffered deteriorations in mental state, were the most likely to have engaged in such behaviour.

---

32 Home Office Circular 66/90 (Home Office, 1990) reflected growing concern about the treatment of mentally disordered people in the criminal justice system by reiterating the government's policy that mentally disordered offenders should only be prosecuted where it was in the public interest to do so. As generally the more serious the offence, the more likely it is to be in the public interest to prosecute, this may explain why reconvictions for more serious offences have remained fairly constant despite a drop in reconviction rates for all offences.

9 Other harmful incidents and concerns about risk

It was clear from studying patients' MHU files that some became involved in incidents that either caused or threatened harm to others and for which (for a variety of reasons) they were never subsequently convicted. Similarly, a recent study which examined the conditional discharge system (Dell and Grounds, 1995) found that seven per cent of a sample of conditionally discharged patients had reportedly been involved in either serious (or potentially serious) violence against others, or arson, for which they were not convicted.

Furthermore, patients' files not uncommonly contained evidence of supervisors expressing fears or concerns to the Home Office about the degree of risk presented by particular patients.

While proven occurrences of reoffending (as represented by reconvictions) were the principal outcomes of interest, information was also collected on these other incidents and concerns. As this aspect of the data collection required using patients' files, information was only available for the 370 conditionally discharged patients.

Because of the obvious link between such behaviours and concerns and considerations of risk, information was collected on any incident where a patient either reportedly caused some injury (or nearly caused serious injury) to another person, or, in cases where the incident had not caused or directly threatened harm, where fears were still expressed by a supervisor about risk in the light of the incident. The latter criterion ensured the inclusion of alleged non-aggressive sexual offences or incidents of attempted fire-setting, which were often viewed with understandable concern by supervisors even though no physical injury was caused to others. The cases of threatening behaviour (see Table 9.1 overleaf) all involved either threats with a weapon or threats to kill.

This categorisation was deliberately restrictive, being intended just to capture those incidents where there was at least some evidence that they had occurred and there was actual or potential harm to others. Alleged incidents of aggressive behaviour – including some attempted assaults - where there was no evidence of injury and the supervisor did not express concern about the incident, were excluded. Incidents which were subsequently proved to be unfounded (for example, where the complainant later admitted that the allegation was false) were also excluded.

Harmful incidents

Thirteen per cent of conditionally discharged patients (n=48) were reportedly involved in various kinds of harmful incidents. As some patients were involved in more than one such alleged incident, the following analysis considers only the most serious incident in each case.

The incidents

Table 9.1 shows the nature of these incidents.

Table 9.1 The most serious reported incidents

Nature of reported incident	%	N
Serious violent assault	6	3
Other violent assault	56	27
Rape or buggery	4	2
Other sexual offence	17	8
Arson	6	3
Threatening behaviour	10	5
		N=48

Note: due to rounding, percentages do not sum to 100

Twenty-nine of these incidents reportedly resulted in some actual injury to the victim, which was serious in two cases. Two other incidents nearly resulted in serious injury (although no injury was apparently caused), and nine others involved threatening or aggressive behaviour (including three assaults where it was not clear whether the victim was hurt). Two of the arson incidents caused damage that was potentially serious. There was no injury caused or threatened in four incidents (all of a sexual nature). The degree of reported harm was not known in two cases.

In nine of the 45 cases where an immediate victim could be identified, the victim was either a partner or family member, and in 12 cases an acquaintance. The victim was an official of some sort (e.g. doctor, nurse or police officer) in 16 cases, and a stranger in eight cases. The three cases without immediate victims were those where the alleged incident was one of fire-setting. The relatively large proportion of victims in the 'official' category reflects the fact that a number of these reported incidents took place in hospitals where the patient was either currently admitted or attending an out-patient appointment.

In 29 per cent of the incidents, a similarity to the index offence was commented upon either by supervisors or the Home Office. As with the reconvictions data, the numbers were too small to allow meaningful statistical analysis, but it was noted that six of the ten patients reportedly involved in sexual incidents had a sexual index offence, all three of the arson incidents patients had an index offence of arson, while the index offence of 25 of the 35 patients (71%) allegedly involved in violent or threatening incidents was a violent one.

There was a significant association between involvement in these reported incidents and reconviction for a serious offence: 15 per cent of the patients involved were reconvicted of a serious offence, compared to just four per cent of patients not reportedly involved in such incidents. Furthermore, those patients with a criminal record featuring either violent or sexual offences prior to the index offence were significantly more likely to have been involved in such incidents than those without such a criminal history (18% versus 9%).

Patients who were described at some stage as causing problems with their supervision were significantly more likely to have been reportedly involved in these harmful incidents than those who did not cause such difficulties: 26 per cent versus eight per cent. In addition, nearly a quarter (24%) of those whose mental state deteriorated during discharge to the point where some psychiatric intervention was required were involved in these incidents, compared to just five per cent of those whose mental state did not deteriorate - also a statistically significant difference. In 42 per cent of these incidents, there was evidence that the patient's mental state appeared to have worsened, or be worsening, at the time of the incident.

Those in the psychopathic disorder and mental impairment categories were slightly more likely than the mentally ill to be involved in incidents (16% of PD and 14% of mental impaired patients, compared to 12% of mentally ill patients). This variation was not statistically significant however.

Ninety per cent of those involved in the incidents (n=43) were male. The patients involved were also significantly younger when discharged from hospital than those not involved: nearly 36 years versus 41 years.

Patients who were described at some stage as having misused either drugs or alcohol were much more likely to have been involved in these incidents than those patients without such problems (33% versus 7%). Over a third of the incidents were said to have involved either drink or drugs.

Black patients were significantly more likely to have been involved in harmful incidents than white or Asian patients (26% versus 11% and 8% respectively).

The response

Although these incidents were not legally proven, generally there seemed to be little doubt that they had occurred (for example, the victim had to receive medical treatment, or the incident was witnessed). In five cases the perpetrator was initially charged but the prosecution was subsequently dropped, usually because the victim refused to press his or her complaint. In another 13 cases, the patient was arrested but not charged. In some of the other cases, the police were called but no arrest was made.

In 37 cases, a supervisor expressed apprehension about the degree of risk posed by the patient following the incident in question; and the Home Office sometimes declared concern in cases where the supervisor had not.

While only a few of the incidents resulted in arrest or prosecution, over a third of the patients involved (n=17) were recalled because of their behaviour and a further six patients were admitted to hospital on a non-recall basis. Eleven other patients received some other form of psychiatric intervention, such as (increased) medication or increased psychiatric supervision. There was no psychiatric or criminal justice intervention in five cases: all were cases where the incident was either felt by supervisors not to have been particularly serious or out of character for a patient whose rehabilitation was otherwise proceeding well.

Discussion

It is difficult to assess the significance of these incidents. As they did not result in conviction, strictly they should be seen just as reported and unproven. The fact that some incidents did not lead to prosecution or recall to hospital implies that they were not perceived as being particularly serious by the police, CPS or the Home Office. Furthermore, it appeared that some of the incidents were triggered by significant provocation or even assault. On the other hand, these incidents caused or threatened harm to others, and the association between the incidents and both previous convictions and reconvictions suggests that they may have been indicative of a patient's propensity for offending behaviour.

The difficulty of deciding what degree of importance to attach to these incidents is emphasised by the fact that in nearly a quarter of them there was no evidence that a supervisor subsequently expressed concerns about risk. Yet those involved in harmful incidents were more than three times as likely to have caused their supervisor concern about risk (on another occasion to the incident itself) than those not involved in such incidents (77% versus 24%) – although, of course, this association may say as much about the supervisor's view of the patient's behaviour as about the behaviour itself.

As Dell and Grounds (1995) suggest, both national policy towards the prosecution of mentally disordered offenders, as well as local police and CPS practice, would have had an effect on whether a particular incident was prosecuted. The fact that the victim was often either acquainted with the offender or acting in an official capacity towards him or her, and thus may have been unwilling to press charges, could account for the low rate of subsequent criminal justice response: certainly, arrest (and prosecution) was proportionally most common in incidents where the victim was a stranger.

At least some of the incidents took place in hospitals or mental health hostels, with the victims being fellow patients or residents. Crichton (1995), discussing violence committed by psychiatric in-patients, suggests that medical staff tend not to report the great majority of assaults by patients to the police, while Sayce (1995) argues that the courts make it difficult to prosecute violence against psychiatric patients by being unwilling to accept psychiatric patients as witnesses.

Concerns about risk

In nearly a third of conditional discharge cases (n=115) a supervisor expressed concern about the possible risk posed by the patient on occasions separate to any reoffending or harmful incidents.

In 86 per cent of these cases the concern was general, based, for example, on circumstances arising that were similar to those surrounding the index offence. In 43 per cent of cases, however, the basis for the concern included specific incidents, including a few cases where allegations were made about harmful behaviour by the patient but quickly retracted, or subsequently proved to be false (and so were not categorised as harmful incidents).

Factors that were most strongly and significantly associated with supervisors expressing concerns about risk were: instability in mental state; causing supervisory difficulties; and problems with drug or alcohol misuse. Younger offenders caused more concern than older ones - the average age at discharge for those who caused their supervisors concern was nearly 37 years, compared to 41 years for those who did not cause concern.

Men were more likely than women to cause concerns, as were those who experienced difficulties in socialising with others. However, neither of these latter two factors achieved statistical significance. Nor was there any significant variation between the different disorder categories, with approximately a third of all three main groups causing their supervisors concern about risk.

The response to these concerns varied. While the Home Office were informed, the concerns were not always reported in such a way as to suggest that the supervisor wished further action to be taken: in some cases, for example, matters causing the supervisor concern were reported some time after the event. Nevertheless, in a third of these cases the patient was recalled to hospital, and over one-sixth of these expressions of concern led to the patient being admitted to hospital on a non-recall basis. In a few cases, patients' conditions of discharge were modified in the light of the concerns. However, in a fifth of these cases, no action further to reporting the matter to the Home Office was taken.

While worries or concerns do not necessarily prove risk (as Grounds (1995) has emphasised), supervisors were understandably very wary of, and sensitive to, any signs that might have indicated danger to others, and such concerns could be taken as evidence of the supervisory process working well. In many cases the causes for concern were either isolated incidents (of which the supervisor may even have received an incorrect or uncertain account), or simply circumstances arising that may have raised the patient's level of risk in his or her supervisor's eyes although nothing untoward actually occurred. Nonetheless, the association between these concerns and reconvictions for a serious offence approached statistical significance: nine per cent of those patients causing concern were reconvicted for a serious offence, compared to four per cent of those not causing concern.

Key points

- Thirteen per cent of conditionally discharged patients were reportedly involved in incidents causing or threatening harm to others that did not result in conviction. Almost half of these patients were admitted to hospital (mostly on recall) as a result of these incidents. There was a significant association between these incidents and being reconvicted of a serious offence.

- In addition, nearly a third of those conditionally discharged caused their supervisors concerns or fears about the risk they posed to others.

10 Recall to hospital

Under Section 42(3) of the MHA 1983, the Home Secretary has the power to recall to hospital any conditionally discharged restricted patient about whom there is concern. Such a power is entirely discretionary and the basis for recall will vary. Formerly, the degree of danger that a patient might present was the key factor, with the Home Office/DHSS Guidance to Supervisors (1987) adding that, given the patient's history of dangerous behaviour, minor problems or failures might be sufficient to raise such concerns. However, the ruling in the *Kay v United Kingdom* case (1994) has established that evidence of a relapse in the patient's mental state (which may present a risk to others) is now the only legitimate reason for recall[33].

A quarter of (n=91) of the sample of 370 conditionally discharged offenders were recalled to hospital at some stage during the study period: 72 were recalled once, 16 were recalled twice, and three people on three or more occasions. This incidence of recall is commensurate with that reported elsewhere: a quarter of Dell and Grounds' (1995) sample were recalled, and recent Home Office figures (Home Office, 1997b) report that 23% of all restricted patients first discharged between 1987 and 1990 were recalled to hospital by the end of 1995. The following analysis focuses predominantly upon first recall.

Which patients were recalled?

Those discharged by MHRTs were more likely to be recalled than those discharged by the Home Secretary (27% compared to 21%), although the difference was not statistically significant. There was no difference in recall rates between the three main MHA categories, nor the sexes, with a quarter of each category and each gender being recalled. Although proportionately more black patients (33%) were recalled than white patients (23%) or patients from Asian or other ethnic groups (15%), the difference was not statistically significant (possibly due to the small numbers involved). This difference is probably connected to the fact that black patients were the most likely to have been described by their supervisors as having caused problems with supervision.

---

33 In this case, the European Court held that before a restricted patient could be recalled to hospital, there had to be current evidence of the existence of mental disorder. This ruling is thought likely to have a significant impact upon the use of recall.

There was also no association between the category of a patient's index offence and whether or not he or she was recalled.

However, the relationship between a patient causing problems with supervision and being recalled was strongly significant. In addition, not only were those patients whose mental state deteriorated to the point where psychiatric intervention was required significantly more likely to be recalled (52%) versus 5% of those who did not require such intervention), but patients who had a history of psychiatric treatment (prior to the restriction order) were also significantly more likely to be recalled than those without such a history.

Given the link between dangerousness and recall, it was not surprising that there was a significant association between being recalled and causing supervisors concerns about risk: 54 per cent of those who caused such concerns were recalled compared to 12 per cent of those who did not. There was also a significant link between recall and reportedly being involved in harmful incidents: 67 per cent of those reportedly involved were recalled, compared to 18 per cent of patients not involved.

While only the Home Office can actually order recall, it was apparent in 72 per cent of first recalls that it was a supervisor who initially suggested or requested recall and the Home Office in the remaining 28 per cent. Only just over half of the 91 people first recalled were living in the community when recalled – the remainder were either already in hospital on a non-recall admission or, in a few cases, in prison.

Half the patients were recalled to RSUs, a third to local hospitals, and the remainder to special hospitals.

Reasons for first recall

In most cases a number of reasons were given. Concern about mental state appeared to be the most common reason (in 63% of cases), followed, both in 50 per cent of cases, by disruptive or worrying conduct (causing severe problems in place of residence, for example) and a significant concern about possible dangerousness. Not co-operating with the terms of supervision (including failure to take medication) was another reason commonly given (in 43% of cases), as were social problems or crises faced by the patient (in 26%). Of the 71 recalled offenders known to be on medication, refusal or failure to take their medication was a factor in nearly a third of their recalls. Psychiatric and supervisory problems created concern because they were thought to be an indication of a growing possibility that a patient might harm others. Sometimes the patient's conduct (such as failure to meet with supervisors) constituted an actual breach of their conditions of discharge.

Overall, 40 per cent of those described as having a problem with either alcohol or drug misuse at some stage during conditional discharge were recalled, compared to just 20 per cent of those who did not have such problems. There was evidence that alcohol or drugs were involved in the behaviour that led to the recall decision in nearly a quarter of all first recalls.

Reported incidents of (actually or potentially) dangerous behaviour were implicated in nearly a third of recalls. Alleged involvement in more petty offending (such as theft) was a factor in a few cases. Of those for whom dangerous behaviour was reported, four were subsequently convicted and another four were prosecuted but either not convicted or the prosecution was later dropped. There was no difference between MHRT and Home Office discharges in terms of dangerous behaviour being a reason for recall. The recall of PD patients however was significantly more likely to have been prompted by dangerous behaviour than that of non-PD patients: 48 per cent versus 25 per cent.

'Dangerous behaviour' recalls were significantly more likely also to have involved alcohol or drugs than were other recalls – 39 per cent compared to 14 per cent. However, the numbers here were very small.

In seven cases, the patients appeared to be recalled primarily to regulate the fact that they were already in hospital (and reassert Home Office control over the case), without any suggestion of dangerous behaviour (or even the threat of it) playing a part in the recall decision.

Mental state at first recall

It appeared that the mental state of nearly two-thirds (63%) of those recalled was worsening at the time of recall. There was more likely to be evidence of deterioration in the case of the mentally ill than in the case of the psychopathically disordered or the mentally impaired. There were concerns about the person's mental state, but no clear evidence of deterioration, in a further 11 per cent of cases. In the remaining 26 per cent, the person's mental condition was either not known, or was thought to be stable. Of course, in cases where patients refused to meet their supervisors it was very difficult to obtain evidence of mental state.

Further recalls

Nineteen people were recalled on more than one occasion. As with first recalls, the most common reason for these further recalls was concern about mental state, followed by a perception that there was a serious possibility of dangerous behaviour or disruptive conduct from the patient.

Reported dangerous behaviour featured in five of these further recalls, although in only one case was a person later convicted as a result of this behaviour.

In over half the 19 cases, some failure or refusal to co-operate with the conditions of discharge was a reason for recall.

Discharge from recall

By the end of the study, just over three-quarters of first recall patients (n=69) were no longer in hospital. Sixty had been conditionally discharged (46 by MHRT, 14 by the Home Office) and five had been absolutely discharged. Two patients had died, one had been convicted and remitted to prison, and one patient was discharged illegally by the RMO (although he was later readmitted to hospital).

In 53 of these 69 cases, the degree of mental disorder was not thought to warrant further detention in hospital. In another three cases, there was said to be no mental disorder within the meaning of the MHA 1983. Detention was thought not to be necessary for the safety or protection of others in 29 cases. Other reasons were also sometimes given for discharge, such as a patient's old age, or the fact that they were suffering from a terminal illness.

Of the 19 people who were recalled more than once, ten had been discharged from these further recalls by the end of the study period. This gave a total of 31 people who had not been discharged from recall by the end of the study period.

Time spent on recall

The average amount of time spent recalled was just over 21 months (median of 11 months)[34]. The periods ranged from one month to over seven years. For those 50 patients who were only recalled once and were discharged again during the study period, the average period of recall detention was 15 months.

---

34 Counting from date of recall to the end of the study period (31 December 1994) for those who had not been discharged by that date.

Key points

- A quarter of the conditionally discharged patients were recalled to hospital during the study period.

- The reasons most commonly given for recall were concern about mental state, concern about actually or potentially dangerous behaviour, or disruptive behaviour. The connecting factor appeared to be fears that the patient was beginning to behave in a way that could eventually lead to others being harmed.

- Not surprisingly, those patients who were described by supervisors as creating problems with supervision or causing concerns about risk were the most likely to be recalled. PD patients were more likely than non-PD patients to be recalled on grounds of reported dangerous behaviour.

- Many of those recalled had been discharged from hospital again by the end of the study period, although a third had not.

- Recall often resulted in quite lengthy periods of further detention: the average length of time spent on recall by the end of the follow-up period was nearly two years.

11 Interviews with MHRT members and MHU staff

Introduction

Semi-structured interviews were carried out with eight MHRT members (drawn from two of the four regional tribunal areas), and five members of the Home Office's Mental Health Unit (MHU). Respondents were selected on the basis of their experience and knowledge of dealing with restriction order cases. They were asked questions on a variety of topics relating primarily to the discharge from hospital and subsequent management in the community of restricted patients. The views that they expressed were, of course, individual ones and not necessarily representative of their respective organisations.

Roles

Respondents were asked about their role in the restriction order system and the relationship with others working in that system.

MHRT members

Tribunal members saw MHRTs as having a vital role in providing a statutory review of the appropriateness of continuing detention. The balance of the MHRTs' composition was felt to be good, with its lay, medical and legal members each contributing a different type of expertise and perspective. The legal member's role as tribunal president was seen as being particularly significant, as he or she controlled proceedings and set the tone of the hearing. One respondent said that he thought presidents were notably cautious about discharging patients. The important role of the medical member in assessing the patient before the tribunal hearing was also highlighted. One lay member, referring to the medical member's expertise in questioning the RMO, said: "in some ways they do almost have the power for changing the course of the tribunal". One medical member said that his opinion of the patient's fitness for discharge only rarely changed after his preliminary visit. Nonetheless, it was generally stressed that no one member's input was any greater than another when it came to deciding upon the evidence.

The Home Office's role in representing and protecting the public was acknowledged, as was the collective knowledge and experience of the MHU (a theme also repeatedly developed by MHU staff). By and large it was felt that the Home Office did a difficult job well, although there was some frustration expressed at the length of time that the Home Office took to come to decisions in restricted cases (which some tribunal members saw as stemming from the Home Office's cautious approach). One view was that the Home Office's duty to the public inevitably lent a political element to their decisions.

Tribunal members' views of RMOs were mostly very positive. Understandably, the RMO's evidence to the tribunal was seen as very influential and important. Rather more doubt was expressed about evidence provided by doctors acting as independent psychiatrists. While any additional information of good quality was said to help decision-making, independent psychiatric reports were sometimes criticised for not offering sufficient concrete assistance, with one tribunal member commenting: "it seems to me that an independent report is not terribly helpful if there's no practical outcome as a result of that report". Concern was also expressed about the adversarial way in which patients' legal representatives sometimes used reports from independent psychiatrists, not disclosing unfavourable ones to the tribunal.

MHU staff

MHU staff stressed that their role arose directly from Part III of the MHA 1983 and amounted to an audit of the evidence of restricted patients' progress from the perspective of public protection.

Public reaction was acknowledged as being a consideration in decision-making. The accountability of MHU decision-making to the public (via the minister) was widely emphasised. In contrast, MHRTs were seen as less directly accountable. However, MHRTs were still described as "performing the same function, but differently" from the Home Office, with the Home Office considering discharge on the basis of a "rolling review" while MHRTs considered discharge on the basis of a "snapshot hearing". While each body was required to look at both the patient's rights and public safety, it was suggested that MHRTs concentrated more on the former and the Home Office more on the latter, leading to a "constructive tension" between the two organisations.

As some tribunal members had also noted, MHU staff emphasised that both the Home Office and the MHRTs were independent decision-making bodies, and so their relationship, although necessarily close, was formally at 'arm's length'. This notion of the different roles and yet inter-relatedness of the various actors within the restriction order system was also highlighted when MHU staff discussed the Home Office's relationship with doctors. As the MHU could only interpret and assess the expert information supplied to them, they were reliant upon the doctors. Doctors were broadly classified either as those who worked well with the Home Office (as one MHU respondent put it: "in a dialogue, but not a cosy relationship"), or those who seemed to feel encumbered and constrained by the Home Office's involvement. While there was some sympathy expressed for the doctors' obvious frustration at delays caused by perceived "bureaucratic inertia", the speed and quality of Home Office decisions were said to be at least partly dependent upon the sufficiency of the clinical information supplied to the MHU.

MHU respondents tended to convey more of a corporate approach to their work than the tribunal members, although this may have been due in part to the fact that they were interviewed in groups (unlike the MHRT members). Nevertheless, it was clear that the collective experience and knowledge that MHU possess is an important part of their decision-making capability.

Length of stay in hospital

MHU members emphasised that there was no 'tariff' requirement dictating how long patients would spend in hospital before the Home Office would be prepared to consider their release. Every case was dealt with on its merits, with the central consideration always being whether the patients could be safely managed in the community. One MHU respondent did think, however, that the Home Office's preference for a patient being fully tested in different environments before discharge might possibly be construed as a kind of tariff.

Some MHRT respondents, particularly the legal members, did seem concerned about the issue of proportionality. One legal member admitted that when a RMO recommended discharge within a short time of a restriction order being imposed, he was inclined to think, "well, what would he [the patient] have got had there been a tariff sentence?". A medical member added that in cases which involved a serious offence, he anticipated a lengthy minimum period of treatment and supervision – in fact, "some sort of tariff element". Conversely, there was disquiet about cases where patients had ended up in the hospital system for many years, even though originally convicted of a relatively minor offence – although this was seen principally as a feature of restriction orders made before the introduction of the 'serious harm' requirement in the 1983 MHA.

The process of discharge from hospital

MHU staff said that, typically, a case discharged with the consent of the Home Secretary was one which had run the full range of testing, in successively lessening levels of security. This process should have provided an understanding on the part of both the patient and his/her carers of the mental disorder, the offending behaviour, and the relationship between them. An important feature is, of course, that Home Office discharge decisions are entirely discretionary.

MHRTs on the other hand, operating under the statutory discharge criteria of Section 72 of the MHA 1983, have less discretion in their decision-making in relation to restricted patients. As one tribunal member put it: "the question, quite simply, is does the patient fulfil the criteria [for discharge]? If the answer is yes, then he must be discharged".

This lack of discretion on the tribunal's part led one MHU respondent to suggest that the most notorious cases are thus more likely to end up being discharged by a MHRT than by the Home Secretary, simply because the MHRT has less leeway in its decision-making. MHU members said that in difficult or high profile cases they would often call upon the expertise of the Home Office's Advisory Board on Restricted Patients.

Nevertheless, MHRT members mentioned that even within the legal criteria there was some room for flexibility, particularly when considering whether continuing detention was "appropriate" (Section 72(1)(b)(i), MHA 1983). One legal member said that while he would tend to look "beyond the immediate and narrow agenda [of the statutory criteria]", he would not make any decision that "you would not care to confess if you were hearing your reasons taken to pieces in the Divisional Court or the Court of Appeal. I simply mean that you are facing a human problem".

The 'double negative' element to Sections 72 and 73[35] was frequently mentioned by MHRT and MHU members alike as being cumbersome and rather confusing (particularly for patients), although it was identified by some as serving the purposes of caution.

---

35   Section 72(1)(b) says that a MHRT should direct a patient's discharge if it is satisfied that the patient is not then suffering from a mental disorder of a nature or degree which makes continued detention appropriate, or that it is not necessary for the patient's health and safety or the protection of others that the patient should receive treatment in hospital. Section 73(1)(b) adds that any discharge should be absolute if the MHRT is satisfied that it is not appropriate for the patient to remain liable to recall. This effectively puts the patient in the position of having to prove that he or she is not currently suffering from a disorder to a degree requiring hospital detention, and allows the tribunal to refuse discharge on grounds of the 'double negative' (ie. not satisfied that the patient is not suffering), which writers such as Peay (1989) have argued is a conceptually easier position to reach than the tribunal having to satisfy itself that the patient was still suffering from the requisite degree of disorder before refusing discharge.

Assessment of risk

Risk assessment was identified by both MHRT and MHU members as being central to any decision to discharge restricted patients. Some MHU members suggested that while MHRTs do have a responsibility for public safety, the nature of the statutory criteria they were employing meant they were guided more by mental health issues. But the tribunal members all stressed the caution with which they looked at discharging restricted patients and noted the difficulties of managing the tension between a patient's and society's interests. Risk was said always to be a consideration when hearing restricted cases. One legal member commented: "you could not conduct a tribunal properly without considering it".

Although the wording of Section 72(1)(b) indicates that restricted patients can be discharged without reference to public safety, tribunal members felt that considerations of risk would be a component not only of the *appropriateness* of continuing detention, but also when considering the *degree* of the disorder. However, cases where the patient did not seem to require detention on health grounds and yet still appeared to pose a risk to others were noted as being particularly difficult.

Discussing the process of actually assessing risk, many respondents mentioned factors that they thought might elevate risk, often mentioning psychopathic disorder and previous paedophile offences. Although MHU staff had the benefit of clearly defined procedures for assessing risk and a body of collective information on restricted patients contained in Home Office files, tribunal members stressed that risk assessment had to be based on the circumstances of each individual case. One tribunal member noted that the difficulties of assessing risk (particularly for patients securely detained in hospital) could lead to a presumption against discharge: "the danger of course is that because risk is so difficult to assess, you won't let *anybody* go because they might do something".

Some tribunal members did mention the difficulty of having to form a 'snapshot' assessment of risk. One commented: "we've got to base that [the assessment of risk] on what we see on the day". However members also mentioned the value to the assessment of risk of the medical member's preliminary visit, which afforded him or her the important opportunity to talk to the care team. Furthermore, the legal members stressed that assessing risk was always an integral part of their work as judges.

Respondents generally acknowledged that effective supervision in the community was vital, as this could reduce (or even negate) the influence of many risk factors, especially if compliance with medication was a key issue. The importance of the continual nature of risk assessment and management was emphasised by MHU staff in particular, based on a recognition both that levels of risk could change over time and circumstance and that all risk could not be eliminated. One MHU member said: "nor do we have any illusions that there is ever a 100 per cent safe discharge decision, because apart from anything else, the link between the mental disorder and the offence may not be total". Many of the tribunal members mentioned cases where they had deferred discharge in order to ensure that the proper support services could be established so as to satisfy themselves that any risk posed by the patient could be effectively managed following discharge from hospital.

Home Office representation at MHRTs

Some tribunal members – most notably the legal members – wished that the Home Office would be legally represented more often at MHRT hearings (although it was acknowledged that in the majority of cases there was no need for this). One legal member thought that this would not make tribunal hearings more adversarial (widely seen as a disadvantage), but rather more "three dimensional" (as he described it), allowing a fuller testing of the evidence.

However, MHU members were opposed to the idea of increased Home Office representation, which at present is only undertaken in cases where the Home Office is very concerned about the possibility of discharge. Aside from the significant resource implications, it was felt that greater Home Office representation could increase the adversarial nature of tribunal hearings, might encourage too much discussion of the management of cases (which would be irrelevant to the real purpose of the hearing) and, furthermore, might threaten the independence of MHRTs. They did feel that Home Office representation, when necessary, should be undertaken by a lawyer who could cross-examine effectively, rather than by a civil servant.

Also discussed was the written Home Office statement which is submitted to the tribunal. Tribunal members felt that the statement was often too negative and too predictably formulaic (which in turn was said to lessen its impact) and that the Home Secretary's observations were often insufficiently justified. MHU staff were aware of the presentational effect of this point (i.e. that the Home Secretary's statement never endorsed discharge) but they added that this was inevitable because if the Home Secretary was satisfied that discharge was appropriate, he/she would have authorised it using his/her own powers. The main purpose of the comments section of the Home Secretary's statement was described as therefore being to ensure that the tribunal was aware of the reasons why he/she had not done so.

Furthermore, MHU staff also had in mind the mutual independence of the two decision-making bodies. They said that the Home Office was not seeking to submit its own decision-making processes for scrutiny but responding to the MHRT's requirement for material to inform its own, separate deliberations.

Perhaps the most significant criticism of the Home Office statement was that the information on the index offence that it provided, while often clear and objective, was sometimes insufficiently detailed. Although MHU members did note the difficulty of trying to supply only objective information (witness statements, for example, could often be partial), this was acknowledged as an issue of concern – especially given the emphasis in recent inquiry hearings on the importance of full and accurate information on the index offence being available (see the Andrew Robinson (Blom-Cooper et al., 1995) and Jason Mitchell (Blom-Cooper, 1996) inquiries, for example).

MHRT hearings

The degree of formality and adversarialism associated with tribunal hearings was discussed. Most tribunal members thought that, the necessary legal framework and formality of procedure aside, the tribunals were quite informal, which was good as it tended to put the patient at his/her ease. There was a view that the degree of formality depended largely upon the attitude of the particular tribunal president, although the legal members who were interviewed found the tribunals more relaxed than court hearings. As one put it: "unlike in a court where you're so remote from them [the patients], here you are sitting face to face and dealing on a very informal basis".

Everyone agreed that it was undesirable for tribunals to become adversarial. MHRT hearings were supposed to be based on an inquisitorial model. One tribunal member said: "it [our title] means what it says: we are reviewing the position". Many respondents did feel that the increased representation of patients by solicitors had led to a more adversarial tone in tribunal hearings. Particular problems identified were the non-disclosure of psychiatric reports prepared for patients' solicitors and the way that some legal representatives attempted to enhance their client's case by challenging the Home Office's position. Nonetheless, one counter-argument, made by a tribunal president, was that increased legal representation "meant no-one could get away with an empty assertion".

There was a clear difference between the two sets of respondents on the issue of the extent of the tribunal's interest in a restricted case. Tribunal members tended to want more powers for MHRTs to become involved in a case's management, such as having the power to direct leave or transfer (subject to clinical agreement), or at least make more substantively meaningful recommendations. However, one member said that there was little point in tribunals having powers of transfer if there were insufficient resources to facilitate this. A number of tribunal members expressed concern about resources, one saying that: "the effectiveness of this whole system…is very much affected by an absence of resources. I have no doubt that some people are being discharged because there's nowhere effective we can send them". He thought that inappropriate placements upon discharge were likely to have adverse consequences for the patients: "you're going to set them up to fail, aren't you?". Another view was that in some cases there were insufficient stages of security in the system to test patients out fully before discharge.

Given the structure of the current system for overseeing restricted cases, Home Office respondents did not think that tribunals could have a greater say in the management of restricted cases, as they were not statutorily required to look beyond the actual tribunal hearing. There was an acknowledgement that MHRTs had to apply difficult legal criteria, and that they probably did not always have sufficient time, resources or information at their disposal.

Tribunal members, when asked about uniformity and consistency of decision-making tended to give one of two views. On the one hand they argued that it did not matter if different members and different tribunals were asking different types of questions, provided the hearing was administered in a correct and just fashion and covered the information relevant to the particular case. On the other hand, some maintained that while what was really important was that the tribunal was conducted correctly and appropriately for each case, it might be helpful for tribunal members to see their fellow medical, lay or legal members at work to ensure greater uniformity.

The timing of MHRT hearings was an issue of concern for many of the tribunal members. The tribunal had to determine whether or not the hearing occurred at an unusually 'good' or 'bad' time for the patient. It was said that while hearings could have a positive therapeutic effect in that they often informed patients as to what their RMOs had planned for them, equally, hearings could be anti-therapeutic if patients heard unfavourable reports about themselves, especially from their RMOs.

Restricted patients in the community

Both MHU and tribunal members spoke of the advantages that the conditional discharge system conferred, particularly because it enabled treatment as well as supervision to take place. Some tribunal members said that it cushioned the discharge decision. A contrast was drawn with the discharge from hospital of patients detained under Section 3 MHA 1983, some of whom were considered to pose as great a risk as restricted patients, if not greater, and yet for whom available post-discharge supervision was often seen as being limited.

Absolute discharges straight from hospital were discussed briefly. MHRT members thought that because of the benefits (and relatively high degree of freedom for the patient) provided by the conditional discharge, an absolute discharge was generally not advantageous. Most of the examples given regarding the use of absolute discharge concerned patients whom the respondents thought probably should not have been given restriction orders in the first place.

As the Home Office is the body with responsibility for overseeing the supervision of restricted patients in the community, issues relating to reoffending and recall were mostly discussed with MHU staff.

The Home Office attitude to reoffending by discharged restricted patients was made very clear: each case would be considered individually, and "there should be no degree of immunity from prosecution", as one MHU respondent put it, unless it was apparent that the reoffending arose from a deterioration in mental state and it seemed inappropriate that a prosecution should take place. It was said that a consequence of the patient's right to be in the community was their responsibility to be treated as any other citizen when it came to criminal proceedings. Even if a prosecution did not result in a new sentence or order being imposed, it was important for the purposes of future information that an offence should be marked by a conviction.

Although the police and CPS still had to consider whether it was in the public interest to prosecute, MHU respondents thought that sometimes these agencies had not always been that willing to prosecute restricted patients, particularly in cases where the patient had already been recalled to hospital.

Following the European Court ruling in the *Kay v United Kingdom* case (see footnote 55 on page 83), evidence of a relapse in the patient's condition (which may present a risk to others) is now the only reason for recall. There was concern that the *Kay* ruling might weaken the power of recall as a device to protect the public, particularly in the case of patients suffering from psychopathic disorder, where deterioration of mental state can be difficult to assess.

MHU respondents were keen to emphasise that the Home Office would not use the recall power lightly, but that if a patient's mental state was clearly deteriorating then he or she may have to be recalled as they might not realise that they were relapsing. In cases where medical advice was clear and relapse appeared to be associated with risk to others, one MHU respondent commented that "the presumption must be for recall rather than leaving them in the community". Ideally, however, the Home Office would explore a range of options before recall (such as a warning letter to the patient, or encouraging a non-recall hospital admission). In particular, social problems were seen as perhaps being better dealt with by means other than a recall. Although recall is undoubtedly a setback for a patient, one MHU member stressed: "recall is not a failure: it is preventing a failure by preventing a reoffence, so it is a perfectly valid tool for ensuring a patient's continuing well-being and the public's safety as well".

Sometimes, the patient's behaviour which leads to recall may include alleged offending, although MHU respondents stressed that they would want to check the details carefully with supervisors before taking action. One tribunal member noted that in considering the case of a recalled patient seeking re-discharge, the tribunal was effectively being "asked to be a court of trial over the incident of what it was that led to his recall". Another tribunal member, also speaking of alleged incidents, gave an example of a hearing he had sat on where a patient had been recalled for a reported incident of dangerous behaviour which it seemed highly likely he had indeed committed and yet, without any firm evidence of this, and with no impending prosecution, there were insufficient grounds to detain the patient further.

Tribunal members mentioned that information on the progress of discharged restricted patients was not available to them on a formal basis. Currently, one of them described the situation following discharge as one where "you just hope for the best, and hope that you don't read their [the patient's] name in the paper". Most felt that such information would be very useful as it would give them more of a feel for their work to know which patients had (or had not) presented problems following discharge. However, an alternative view was that such information, while interesting, would be of little practical value as each case would still have to be judged individually.

Mental disorder issues

Aspects of dealing with psychopathically disordered patients particularly seemed to trouble respondents.

Tribunal members said that if a PD patient had received the appropriate treatment, had behaved well for a sustained period and presented well at his/her tribunal, then the conclusion had to be drawn that the patient had made progress. Or, as one respondent put it, "don't you have to give him the benefit of the doubt?". Unlike most mentally ill patients, those with psychopathic disorder might not show any signs of their condition at all – in which case, any tribunal would find it difficult to authorise their continuing detention, notwithstanding concerns about public safety. Tribunal members were well aware that the difficulties of assessing psychopathic disorder meant that they could not be certain that problems might not arise again once the patient was out in the community. The particular difficulty of assessing the risk presented by a PD patient while they were securely detained in hospital was mentioned by most tribunal respondents.

MHU members mentioned the problem that psychopathic disorder was a legal, not a clinical definition, and so tended to cover a very heterogeneous range of people and disorders. There was particular concern that supervision for PD patients did not always work successfully. One MHU respondent said of the current arrangements for psychopathically disordered offenders, "there is good reason to improve the service to them". Similarly, one tribunal member suggested that the problems could not be considered to lie solely with the patients but that the system is failing those with psychopathic disorder to the point where the current situation is "unsatisfactory and morally indefensible". Although one MHU member thought that the mere existence of the restriction order might restrain a PD patient's behaviour, an alternative, more pessimistic view was that the restriction order serves no purpose with PD patients unless they reoffended or presented a clear risk and could then be recalled (although this would now be subject to the effects of the *Kay* ruling).

In the light of these difficulties, MHU respondents saw the need for alternatives to the restriction order to be considered, such as the new hospital direction (see footnote 19 on page 42).

A contrast was drawn with mentally ill patients to whom it was felt that the restriction order, with its conditional discharge system, was especially well-suited, particularly if there was a clear association between the illness and the offending. The nature of mental illness made signs of deterioration easier to detect and the importance of medication in most cases of mental illness made compliance with treatment easier to assess. Furthermore, MHU respondents thought that mentally ill patients more often saw their supervisors as being there to help them, whereas many PD patients were said to see supervisors merely as a complication or hindrance to their lives in the community.

Key points

- While there was some variance apparent in how tribunal and MHU members saw each other's roles, reflecting the different aims, ethos, and background of the two organisations, both groups of respondents broadly shared many concerns. These included, for example, the difficulties of assessing risk accurately, problems associated with psychopathic disorder, and the need to ensure the availability of accurate and detailed information about the patient.

- Similarly, both groups of respondents were positive about some of the benefits of the restriction order, such as the conditional discharge system.

- While the Home Office's MHU and the MHRTs take different approaches to achieving an essentially common objective – the safe and effective discharge from hospital of restricted patients – both had developed ways of best achieving that difficult goal: the MHU through their collective experience and knowledge, and the tribunals through the expertise and skills the different MHRT members brought to their work.

12 Discussion

The group of offenders that are the subject of this report represent the more serious end of the spectrum of offending by mentally disordered people. It is worth emphasising that not only are the great majority of offenders not mentally disordered, but also that most mentally disordered offenders do not present a serious risk to others. Under half of one per cent of all sentences passed between 1992 and 1996 were hospital orders, and only around a quarter of the latter were accompanied by a restriction order (Home Office, 1994, 1997c).

However, for those mentally disordered offenders who are believed to pose a serious risk to others, restriction orders play an important part in ensuring that the public is protected from further offending by them and, notwithstanding the fact that courts now have another option for dealing with psychopathically disordered offenders (the hospital direction) under the Crime (Sentences) Act 1997, they are likely to continue to do so. Because of their important role in protecting the public, but also because of their implications both for resources and civil liberties, it is important that attempts are made to assess the value of restriction orders and how effectively they achieve their aims. This report has examined the imposition of restricted hospital orders, the discharge of restricted patients from hospital, and their subsequent progress in the community.

Value and effectiveness

The findings suggest a number of indications of the order's value and effectiveness:

- For the great majority of offenders in the sample, with their history of serious offending and often extensive psychiatric histories, it seemed the only suitable sentence. In most cases, either prison sentences or unrestricted hospital orders would have been inappropriate.

- The reconviction rate for serious offences among those patients discharged was very low. While it cannot be causally shown that this was a result of restriction orders, it seems likely that they played a significant role in many cases.

- An examination of patients' files and interviews with practitioners indicated the particular advantages of the conditional discharge system (for a detailed analysis of this system, see Dell and Grounds, 1995), both in terms of ensuring care and support for patients after their discharge from hospital but also their continuing supervision and recall to hospital if necessary.

- Some interview respondents commented on the value of restriction orders in sharing the responsibility for the appropriate disposal and subsequent management of dangerous mentally disordered offenders between different agencies and decision-makers. It was also suggested that the orders may play an important demonstrative role, with their (usually) indefinite nature helping allay public fears about such offenders.

The considerations of public safety that underpin the decision to impose a restriction order – unlike the hospital order which is imposed for clinical reasons – mean that the order should primarily be judged by forensic criteria. Consequently, while *any* serious reoffending by restricted patients is alarming, it is at least encouraging that only such a small proportion of the sample of discharged patients were reconvicted of serious offences or were involved in other harmful incidents.

This study did not attempt to analyse in detail the nature of a restriction order's social or clinical impact upon patients although it was seen that the majority of the discharged patients responded well to the challenges of resettling into the community, often making notable rehabilitative achievements. Conversely, a number of patients suffered either marked deteriorations in their mental state, harmed themselves, or were victims of offences following their discharge from hospital.

Areas of concern

While the research did not indicate any significant shortcomings in the operation of restricted hospital orders, it did expose some areas of concern:

- There were just a few seemingly anomalous cases where the index offence and offending history did not on the face of things suggest that the offender would be likely to cause serious harm[36]. These may have been examples of a judge imposing a restriction order too readily, as some interviewees suggested, or the psychiatrists involved basing their recommendation of a restriction order more on a desire to ensure treatment after discharge from hospital than an assessment of the risk posed by the offender.

---

36   Although it must be acknowledged that a full assessment of risk would include consideration of a wide range of more qualitative, individualistic factors, details of which could not be readily collected for this study.

- In some cases, more details of reported incidents of dangerous behaviour post-discharge and more information on both the index offence and offending history would have better aided decision-makers.

- There were indications of a need for a continuing, if not increasing, level of dialogue between the Home Office and MHRTs, to ensure that both organisations have a good understanding of the other's position and concerns.

- Although not necessarily a function of the operation of restricted hospital orders, the notably high proportion of black people in the samples is clearly an issue that merits further examination, not least because it follows a number of other studies showing an over-representation of black people compulsorily detained under the Mental Health Act 1983 (see Cope, 1990).

Civil liberties implications

While the research undoubtedly highlights the value of the statutory supervision in the community to which most restricted patients are subject under a conditional discharge, the constraints that the conditions of discharge may place upon patients' freedom of movement (following also what was usually a lengthy period of hospital detention) must be recognised. This is particularly so with recall to hospital – a discretionary measure which was used in the case of one in every four of the sample of discharged patients. Once recalled, these patients spent an average of almost two further years in hospital.

Issues such as recall to hospital and the conditions placed on discharge may arouse understandable concerns about the impact of these orders upon the civil liberties of patients. It has to be accepted that some patients would probably not have reoffended whether or not they had been under a restriction order. At the same time it must be recognised that supervision and recall, along with restrictions on discharge from hospital, are essentially preventative measures which are used primarily to protect the public. We cannot know, for example, what the consequences may have been in some cases had patients not been recalled when they were. This tension between the patient's interests and the demands of public protection is inherent in the restriction order system and was often apparent in the research, not least in the study of the decision to discharge. Both MHU and tribunal members spoke of the caution that inevitably accompanied consideration of discharging restricted patients from hospital[37].

---

37 Writers such as Peay (1989) and Baker (1992,1993) have noted the anomaly inherent in the restriction order: one can only be imposed with reference to protecting the public, whereas the discharge decision does not necessarily involve such considerations (see section 72(1)(b), MHA 1983). However, both MHRT and MHU members said that risk will always be taken into account in the discharge of restricted patients from hospital, suggesting that considerations of risk become interlaced with considerations of a patient's disorder (as Peay, 1989, has noted).

As Walker (1996) points out, equating the 'mistake' of excessively detaining a patient in hospital with the 'mistake' of prematurely discharging or failing to recall a patient who goes on to commit another serious offence is fallacious – they are clearly not the same. This makes any attempt to strike an acceptable balance between society's and an individual's interests yet more difficult. The Floud Committee, which looked at the issue of dangerous offenders (Floud and Young, 1981), suggested that once somebody had done or attempted to do serious harm (as the great majority of offenders in this study had) they forfeited their right to be presumed harmless and could then be dealt with as though potentially harmful, which may include being detained or supervised for preventative reasons. Such would seem to be the case with offenders made subject to restricted hospital orders, upon whom the burden falls subsequently to prove that they no longer pose a risk to others.

Risk and risk assessment

It is clear that the significant demands and constraints that restricted hospital orders place upon patients, as well as their resource-intensiveness, mean that their use can be justified only if employed accurately and appropriately. In terms of imposing the orders, it seemed that the risk posed by an offender was in most cases readily apparent – certainly, the judges interviewed thought so. However, deciding that an offender is a risk to others in the aftermath of a serious offence (as the majority of those in the sample had committed), and thus that a restriction order should be imposed, is arguably easier than determining that the same offender is not a risk to others, and thus may warrant discharge from hospital or the terms of their order altogether, after perhaps many years under restrictions. Understandably, it is these latter decisions, which entail the loosening (or dropping) of restrictions on a patient which tend to attract the most attention.

Yet just as important as the assessment of risk at key decision-making points is the longer-term management of risk. With a restriction order this is emphasised by the usual continuation of restrictions after discharge from hospital. The value this brings is notable. For example, while only a small proportion of those discharged reoffended in a way that harmed others, a significant minority caused concerns about risk they posed. In some cases these concerns were provoked by potentially dangerous behaviour on the patient's part. Without the close supervision provided by the conditional discharge system these incidents may never have been known about and the opportunity for timely intervention lost.

Of course, efforts to improve the accuracy of risk assessments at discharge must still be pursued, but in cases where discharged patients have reoffended seriously, the longer the time since the discharge decision, the more difficult it is to say that the assessment of risk and the decision itself was necessarily flawed. It must be remembered that risk (and thus its assessment and management) is a dynamic factor, changing over time and circumstance. In some cases, factors elevating the level of risk will be specific, situational ones, which perhaps could not even have been anticipated at time of discharge. In this context, it is relevant to note that the average length of time between discharge and reoffending was over two years.

Conclusion

Serious offending by people suffering from mental disorders is a matter of perennial concern. In cases where a mentally disordered offender appears to pose a continuing risk to others this study has indicated that a restricted hospital order can play a central role in controlling or even negating that risk, both through ensuring secure detention in hospital but also (and perhaps more significantly) by focusing considerable resources and scrutiny upon discharge from hospital and the subsequent management and supervision of the patient in the community

Demographic information by diagnosis group — Section 1

		Mental Illness		Psychopathic Disorder		Mental Impairment		Mixed: M.I. + P.D.		Total Sample	
		%	N	%	N	%	N	%	N	%	N
Sex	Male	90	259	79	38	86	18	81	13	88	328
	Female	10	28	21	10	14	3	19	3	12	44
Average age atconviction		32.8 years		26.6 years		25.8 years		30.8 years		31.5 years	
Ethnic Origin	White	63	163	95	40	100	21	80	12	70	236
	Black	27	69	2	1	-	-	13	2	21	72
	Asian	4	11	-	-	-	-	-	-	3	11
	Other	6	15	2	1	-	-	7	1	5	17
Living where:	Own home	50	143	40	19	24	5	50	8	47	175
	Relatives home	21	59	27	13	14	3	19	3	21	78
	Hospital	10	28	8	4	24	5	13	2	11	39
	Other	19	55	25	12	38	8	19	3	21	78
Living with:	On own	43	120	42	20	24	5	44	7	41	152
	Relative/friend	31	86	31	15	24	5	31	5	30	111
	Partner	14	40	10	5	14	3	13	2	14	50
	Other	13	36	17	8	38	8	13	2	15	54
Employment	Working	9	25	27	13	10	2	13	2	11	42
	Studying	1	2	-	-	-	-	-	-	1	2
	Neither	90	256	73	35	90	18	88	14	88	323

Psychiatric history by diagnosis group — Section I

		Mental Illness		Psychopathic Disorder		Mental Impairment		Mixed: M.I. + P.D.		Total Sample	
		%	N	%	N	%	N	%	N	%	N
Previous Treatment	in-patient 2+ occasions	59	169	33	16	38	8	75	12	55	205
	in-patient on 1 occasion	13	37	21	10	19	4	-	-	14	51
	out-patient only	6	16	15	7	19	4	6	1	8	28
	G.P. only	7	20	6	3	-	-	6	1	7	24
	None	15	44	25	12	24	5	13	2	17	63
Average age at first in-patient admission		23.5 years		18.3 years		21.4 years		20.9 years		22.7 years	
Treatment in six months prior to index offence	in-patient	29	81	15	7	30	6	50	8	28	102
	out-patient or G.P.	27	75	21	10	20	4	13	2	25	91
	none	44	124	64	30	50	10	38	6	47	170

Appendix B:

Criminal history by diagnosis group — Section 1

		Mental Illness %	N	Psychopathic Disorder %	N	Mental Impairment %	N	Mixed: M.I. + P.D. %	N	Total Sample %	N
Any previous convictions	Yes	71	205	81	39	81	17	88	14	74	275
Previous convictions for sex or violence	Yes	48	139	54	26	38	8	63	10	49	183
Average age at first conviction		19.1 years		16.1 years		17.5 years		19.0 years		18.5 years	
Previous prison sentence	Yes	38	110	48	23	24	5	63	10	40	148
Average age at first custodial sentence		21.1 years		18.9 years		18.0 years		21.2 years		20.7 years	

Appendix D: Logistic regression analysis of serious reconvictions and harmful incidents — Section 2

In an attempt to predict either serious reconvictions or incidents of harmful behaviour, the most satisfactory model was constructed using the following variables: previous sex offences; problems with supervision (see below); problems with drug or alcohol misuse; and deterioration of mental state to the point where some intervention was required.

As a strong association between predictor variables causes distortion in logistic regression models, the 'causing supervisory difficulties' variable and the 'causing supervisors concerns about risk' variable were combined into a new variable entitled 'problems with supervision'. 'Problem (1)' means that a patient *either* caused difficulties with supervision, *or* caused supervisors concerns about risk, while 'Problems (2)' means that a patient *both* caused supervisory difficulties *and* concerns about risk. Because of its specific nature, the 'problems with drugs or alcohol' variable was kept separate.

The estimated coefficients produced by this model are shown in the table below. Each of these coefficients represent the change in the 'log odds' of serious reconviction or involvement in harmful incidents (i.e. a change in the likelihood of these events occurring) associated with a one-unit increase in a predictor variable, while controlling for all other predictor variables. It can be seen that for all the predictor variables an increase in value is associated with a greater likelihood of serious reconviction/harmful incident.

Logistic regression analysis predicting risk of serious reconvictions and/or harmful incidents

Variable	Coefficient estimate	Standard Error	Wald Statistic	Signif	R
Previous sexual offences and sexual index offence	2.2546	.5066	19.8079	.0000	.2347
Problems with supervision:			15.4164	.0004	.1879
Problem (1)	1.5457	.4406	12.3072	.0005	.1786
Problem (2)	1.7946	.4972	13.0259	.0003	.1847
Problems with drugs or alcohol	1.3555	.3524	14.7961	.0001	.1989
Deterioration in mental state	1.2750	.4406	10.4861	.0012	.1620
Constant	-5.4248	.7374	54.1188	.0000	

Because the size of the units of the predictor variables will affect the size of the coefficient estimate, to obtain a comparable indicator of the effect of the different predictor variables, it is necessary also to look at the Wald statistic and the R statistic. The latter can range in value from -1 to +1 (a positive value indicating that as the variable increases, so does the chances of the event occurring, while a negative value indicates the opposite), and is a measure of the relative (and partial) contribution of each variable to the model.

These statistics show that previous sexually-motivated offending, causing problems with supervision, and misuse of drugs or alcohol are the strongest predictors of serious reconvictions/harmful incidents.

While the overall fit of the model to the data was good (-2 Log Likelihood=230.547, df=351, p=1.000; Model chi-square=92.758, df=5, p=.0000) the greater interest in a model of this kind is likely to be in its ability to predict reoffending.

A fairly crude estimate of the model's overall ability to predict reoffending is given by the following classification table, which categorises cases according to their risk of reconviction (i.e. cases with a risk greater than 50% are predicted to reoffend while those with a risk less than 50% are predicted as not reoffending).

Observed and predicted reconviction rates

	Predicted		
Observed	*Did not reoffend*	*Reoffended*	*% correctly predicted*
Did not reoffend	277	20	93%
Reoffended	29	31	52%
% correctly predicted	91%	61%	Total correctly predicted = 86%

Note: 34 cases were excluded from the analysis because of missing data

Although the successful prediction rate of 86 per cent for the whole model was good, the model's ability to predict those who actually did reoffend was only slightly better than chance (52%).

References

Bailey, J., and MacCulloch, M. (1992). *'Patterns of reconviction in patients discharged to the community from a special hospital: implications for aftercare'*. Journal of Forensic Psychiatry, 3/3, 445–461

Baker, E. (1992). *'Dangerousness. The neglected gaoler: disorder and risk under the Mental Health Act 1983'*. Journal of Forensic Psychiatry, 3/1, 31–52.

Baker, E. (1993). *'Dangerousness, rights, and criminal justice'*. Modern Law Review, 56/4, 528–547.

Blom-Cooper, L., Hally, H., and Murphy E. (1995). *The falling shadow: one patient's mental health care 1978-1993.* London: Duckworth.

Blom-Cooper, L. (1996). *The case of Jason Mitchell: report of the independent panel of inquiry.* London: Duckworth.

Boast, N., and Chesterman, P. (1995). *'Black people and secure psychiatric facilities: patterns of processing, and the role of stereotypes'*. British Journal of Criminology, 35/2, 218–235.

Cope, R. (1990). *'Psychiatry, ethnicity, and crime'*, in Bluglass, R. and Bowden, P. (eds) Principles and practice of forensic psychiatry. London: Churchill Livingstone.

Crichton, J. (1995). *'The response to psychiatric in-patient violence'* in Crichton, J. (ed) Psychiatric patient violence: risk and response. London: Duckworth.

Dell, S., and Grounds, A. (1995). *The discharge and supervision of restricted patients.* Report to the Home Office.

Department of Health (1995). *In-patients formally detained in hospitals under the Mental Health Act 1983 and other legislation, England: 1987-88 to 1992-93.* Statistical Bulletin 1995/4. London: GSS.

Department of Health and Home Office (1996). *Mentally disordered offenders: sentencing and discharge arrangements.* Discussion Paper.

Floud, J., and Young, W. (1981). *Dangerousness and criminal justice.* London: Heinemann.

Grounds, A. (1995). *'Risk assessment and management in clinical context',* in Crichton, J. (ed) Psychiatric patient violence: risk and response. London: Duckworth.

Hepworth, D. (1985). *'Dangerousness and the Mental Health Review Tribunal',* in Farrington, D., and Gunn, J. (eds) Aggression and dangerousness. London: Wiley.

Hodgins, S. (ed) (1993). *Crime and mental disorder.* Newbury Park: Sage.

Home Office and Department of Health and Social Security (1987). *Supervision and after-care of conditionally discharged restricted patients. Notes for the guidance of supervisors.* HO/DHSS.

Home Office (1993). *Prison Statistics: England and Wales 1993.* London: HMSO.

Home Office (1994). *Criminal Statistics: England and Wales 1993.* London: HMSO.

Home Office (1997a). *Statistics of mentally disordered offenders: England and Wales 1995.* Home Office Statistical Bulletin 20/97. London:GSS.

Home Office (1997b). *Restricted patients - reconvictions and recalls by the end of 1995: England and Wales.* Home Office Statistical Bulletin 1/97. London: GSS.

Home Office (1997c). *Criminal Statistics: England and Wales 1996.* London: HMSO.

McGovern, D. and Cope, R. (1987). *'The compulsory detention of males of different ethnic groups, with special reference to offender-patients'.* British Journal of Psychiatry, 150, 505–512.

Monahan, J., and Steadman, H. (1994). *Violence and mental disorder: developments in risk assessment.* Chicago: University of Chicago Press.

Murray, D. (1989). *Review of research on reoffending of mentally disordered offenders.* Home Office Research and Planning Unit Paper 55. London: Home Office.

Peay, J. (1989). *Tribunals on trial. A study of decision making under the Mental Health Act 1983.* Oxford: Clarendon Press.

Ritchie, J., Dick, D., and Lingham, R. (1994). *The report of the inquiry into the care and treatment of Christopher Clunis.* London: HMSO.

Robertson, G. (1989). *'The restricted hospital order'.* Psychiatric Bulletin, 4-11.

Sayce, L. (1995). *'Response to violence: a framework for fair treatment'* in Crichton, J. (ed) Psychiatric patient violence: risk and response. London: Duckworth.

Walker, N. (1991). *'Dangerous mistakes'.* British Journal of Psychiatry, 158, 752-757.

Walker, N. (ed) (1996). *Dangerous people.* London: Blackstone Press

Legal cases

R v Birch (1989) *90 Criminal Appeal Reports, 78-90.*

R v Courtney (1988) *9 Criminal Appeal Reports (sentencing), 404-407.*

R v Gardiner (1967) *1 All England Reports, 895-899.*

Kay v United Kingdom (1994) *Report of the ECHR.*

Publications

List of research publications

The most recent research reports published are listed below. A **full** list of publications is available on request from the Research and Statistics Directorate Information and Publications Group.

Home Office Research Studies (HORS)

176. **The perpetrators of racial harassment and racial violence.** Rae Sibbitt. 1997.

177. **Electronic monitoring in practice: the second year of the trials of curfew orders.** Ed Mortimer and Chris May. 1997.

178. **Handling stolen goods and theft: A market reduction approach.** Mike Sutton. 1998.

179. **Attitudes to punishment: findings from the British Crime Survey.** Michael Hough and Julian Roberts. 1998.

180. **Sentencing Practice: an examination of decisions in magistrates' courts and the Crown Court in the mid–1990's.** Claire Flood-Page and Alan Mackie. 1998.

181. **Coroner service survey.** Roger Tarling. 1998.

182. **The prevention of plastic and cheque fraud revisited.** Michael Levi and Jim Handley. 1998.

183. **Drugs and crime: the results of research on drug testing and interviewing arrestees.** Trevor Bennett. 1998.

184. **Remand decisions and offending on bail: evaluation of the Bail Process Project.** Patricia M Morgan and Paul F Henderson. 1998.

187. **Reducing Offending: An assesment of research evidence on ways of dealing with offending behaviour.** Edited by Peter Goldblatt and Chris Lewis. 1998.

Research Findings

52.	**Police cautioning in the 1990s.** Roger Evans and Rachel Ellis. 1997.

53.	**A reconviction study of HMP Grendon Therapeutic Community.** Peter Marshall. 1997.

54.	**Control in category c prisons.** Simon Marshall. 1997.

55.	**The prevalence of convictions for sexual offending.** Peter Marshall. 1997.

56.	**Drug misuse declared in 1996: key results from the British Crime Survey.** Malcolm Ramsay and Josephine Spiller. 1997.

57.	**The 1996 International Crime Victimisation Survey.** Pat Mayhew and Phillip White. 1997.

58.	**The sentencing of women: a section 95 publication.** Carol Hedderman and Lizanne Dowds. 1997.

59.	**Ethnicity and contacts with the police: latest findings from the British Crime Survey.** Tom Bucke. 1997.

60.	**Policing and the public: findings from the 1996 British Crime Survey.** Catriona Mirrlees-Black and Tracy Budd. 1997.

61.	**Changing offenders' attitudes and behaviour: what works?** Julie Vennard, Carol Hedderman and Darren Sugg. 1997.

62.	**Suspects in police custody and the revised PACE codes of practice.** Tom Bucke and David Brown. 1997.

63.	**Neighbourhood watch co-ordinators.** Elizabeth Turner and Banos Alexandrou. 1997.

64.	**Attitudes to punishment: findings from the 1996 British Crime Survey.** Michael Hough and Julian Roberts. 1998.

65.	**The effects of video violence on young offenders.** Kevin Browne and Amanda Pennell. 1998.

66.	**Electronic monitoring of curfew orders: the second year of the trials.** Ed Mortimer and Chris May. 1998.

67. **Public perceptions of drug-related crime in 1997.** Nigel Charles. 1998.

68. **Witness care in magistrates' courts and the youth court.** Joyce Plotnikoff and Richard Woolfson. 1998.

69. **Handling stolen goods and theft: a market reduction approach.** Mike Sutton. 1998.

70. **Drug testing arrestees.** Trevor Bennett. 1998.

71. **Prevention of plastic card fraud.** Michael Levi and Jim Handley. 1998.

72. **Offending on bail and police use of conditional bail.** David Brown. 1998.

73. **Voluntary after-care.** Mike Maguire, Peter Raynor, Maurice Vanstone and Jocelyn Kynch. 1998.

74. **Fast-tracking of persistent young offenders.** John Graham. 1998.

75. **Mandatory drug testing in prisons – an evaluation.** Kimmett Edgar and Ian O'Donnell. 1998.

Occasional Papers

Evaluation of a Home Office initiative to help offenders into employment. Ken Roberts, Alana Barton, Julian Buchanan and Barry Goldson. 1997.

The impact of the national lottery on the horse-race betting levy. Simon Field and James Dunmore. 1997.

The cost of fires. A review of the information available. Donald Roy. 1997.

Monitoring and evaluation of WOLDS remand prison and comparisons with public-sector prisons, in particular HMP Woodhill. A Keith Bottomley, Adrian James, Emma Clare and Alison Liebling. 1997.

Requests for Publications

Home Office Research Studies and Research Findings can be requested from:

Research and Statistics Directorate
Information and Publications Group
Room 201, Home Office
50 Queen Anne's Gate
London SW1H 9AT
Telephone: 0171-273 2084
Fascimile: 0171-222 0211
Internet: http://www.homeoffice.gov.uk/rsd/rsdhome.htm
E-mail: rsd.ho.apollo@gtnet.gov.uk

Occasional Papers can be purchased from:
Home Office
Publications Unit
50 Queen Anne's Gate
London SW1H 9AT
Telephone: 0171-273 2302

HMSO Publications Centre

(Mail, fax and telephone orders only)
PO Box 276, London SW8 5DT
Telephone orders: 0171-873 9090
General enquiries: 0171-873 0011
(queuing system in operation for both numbers)
Fax orders: 0171-873 8200